GLASGOW'S PATHWAYS

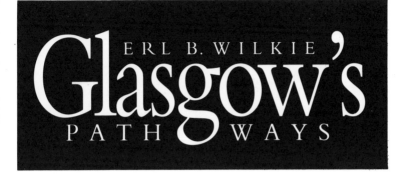

ERL B. WILKIE

Glasgow's PATHWAYS

200 Miles of Running, Cycling
and Walking Routes in and
Around Glasgow

MAINSTREAM
PUBLISHING

EDINBURGH AND LONDON

For Anne and Kirsten

First published in Great Britain in 1993 by
MAINSTREAM PUBLISHING COMPANY (EDINBURGH) LTD
7 Albany Street
Edinburgh EH1 3UG

ISBN 1 85158 222 2

A catalogue record for this book is available from the British Library

Typeset in Janson Text by Servis Filmsetting Ltd, Manchester

Printed in Great Britain by The Cromwell Press, Melksham, Wiltshire

Chequered fields and webs of trees;
whispers of smoke and half-light
on the lochs like
closing eyes.

In the crisp Sunday creases
of the land a toehold of sandstone
nudges through hems of cloud
and people, ghosts on a landscape
green as sap, move off on paths
spread through the hills
like old scars; gingerly,
as though on glass or bones,
or memories,
the purpose transient,
the roads, ritual.

Hugh McMillan, Ritual Roads

Acknowledgments

I am indebted to the following for their help in the preparation of this book: the Planning Departments, Library and Museum Departments and publications of the District Councils of Bearsden and Milngavie, Clydebank, Clydesdale, Cumbernauld and Kilsyth, Cunninghame, Dumbarton, East Kilbride, Eastwood, Falkirk, Glasgow, Kilmarnock and Loudoun, Hamilton, Monklands, Motherwell and Strathkelvin; the British Waterways Board; Sustrans Scotland; the Forestry Commission; and Strathclyde Regional Council Department of Roads. Many thanks also to the many individuals I met along the route who gave me so much local information, and especially to Ian Johnstone for his guided tour of East Kilbride, to Tony Thom for his invaluable help with the maps, and last but not least to Donald Christie for running many miles of research with me.

Contents

Bibliography

Darton, Mike, *Dictionary of Scottish Place Names* (Lochar)

Gordon, J., *Kilsyth History Trail* (Kilsyth Civic Trust)

Herbert, B. W. H., *The Story of Carmunnock* (Carmunnock Preservation Society)

King, E., *People's Palace and Glasgow Green* (Chambers)

MacLean, Fitzroy, *Concise History of Scotland* (Book Club Assocation, London)

McLeod, I., and Gilroy, M., *Discovering the River Clyde* (John Donald)

MacPhail, I. M. M., *Dumbarton Through the Centuries* (Dumbarton Town Council)

Millar, Hugo, *History of Cumbernauld and Kilsyth* (Cumbernauld Historical Society)

Oakley, C. A., *The Second City* (Blackie)

Parker, Derek P., *A History of Elderslie* (CWS Ltd)

Simpson, W. D., *Bothwell Castle* (Historic Scotland, HMSO)

Bridgend, a Scottish Colliery Village, Strathkelvin Mining Project Team

Strawhorn, J., *Ayrshire the Story of a County* (AANHS)

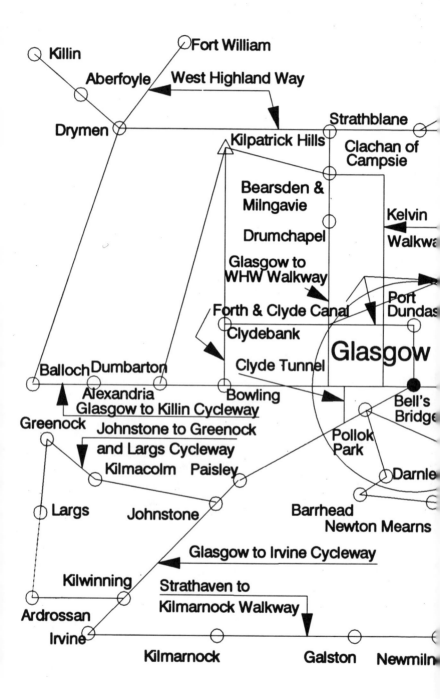

NETWORK OF ROUTES

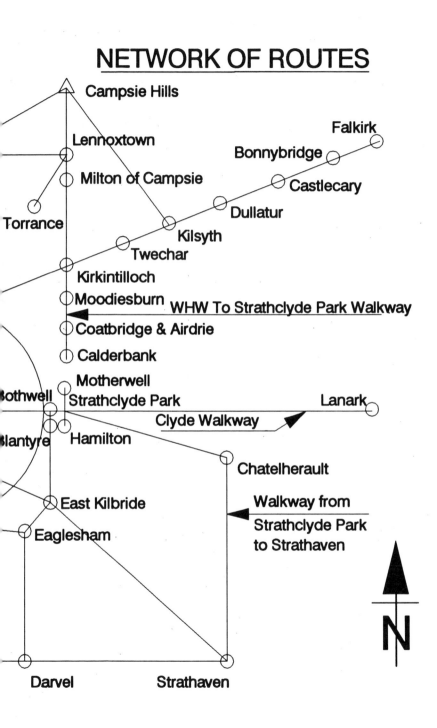

List of Country, Forest, National and City Parks within the network area

The numbers shown relate to the numbers on the map.

Glasgow Parks
1. Glasgow Green
2. Richmond Park
3. Bellahouston Park
4. Pollok Country Park
5. Queen's Park
6. Linn Park
7. Victoria Park
8. Kelvingrove Park
9. Royal Botanical Gardens
10. Maryhill Park
11. Ruchill Park
12. Dawsholm Park

Country Parks
13. Gleniffer Braes Country Park
14. Castle Semple Country Park
15. Lochwinnoch Bird Sanctuary

16. Eglinton Country Park
17. Kelburn Country Park
18. Dean Castle Country Park
19. Balloch Castle Country Park
20. Calderglen Country Park
21. Chatelherault Country Park
22. Strathclyde Country Park
23. Dalzell Country Park
24. Drumpellier Country Park
25. Colzium Park
26. Mugdock Country Park
27. Calendar Park Country Park

National Parks
28. Muirshiel Country Park
29. Queen Elizabeth Forest National Park

Forest Parks
30. Whitelee Forest
31. Lennox Forest

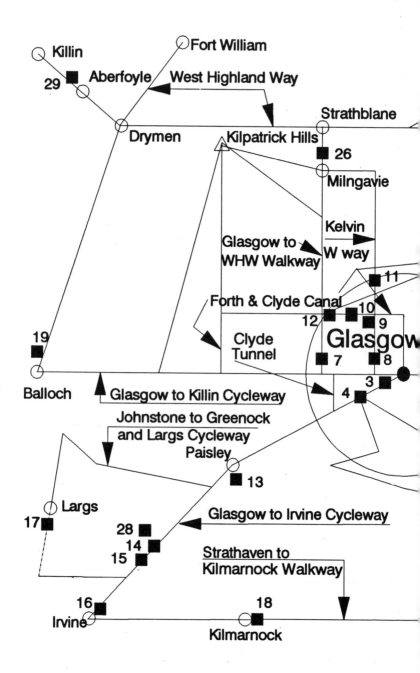

NETWORK - SHOWING COUNTRY PARKS AND GLASGOW PARKS

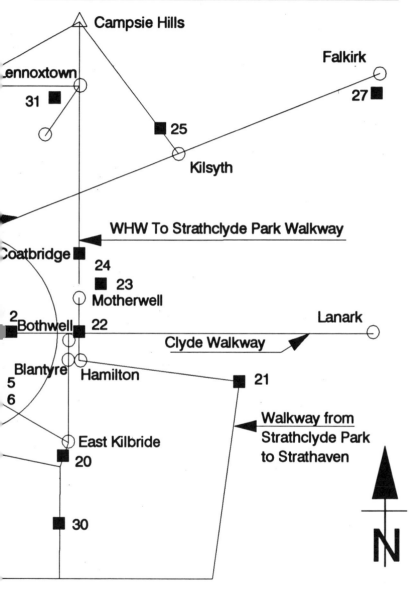

Introduction

For many years now I have been a long-distance runner, having started this sport primarily to keep fit. After giving up playing rugby in my mid-30s, I found I was doing no exercise at all and, as I have a sedentary job, my weight increased at an alarming rate. As I approached 40 I came to the conclusion that if I were not to become another statistic in Scotland's poor health record I should take up a sport and perhaps get a little fitter. But what? I didn't like running – I thought that was boring. What enjoyment could one possibly get from pounding the streets? I had been a runner in my youth (quite a good one, in fact) but that was over short distances such as 100 and 200 yards, and I had enjoyed that until I discovered beer and cigarettes!

It was at this time that marathon mania was sweeping the country: the first Glasgow Marathon had been run with great success and people were starting with much enthusiasm to train for the second, so I thought I would have a go. Dragging my overweight body around the streets was all I had ever thought it would be and more – absolute bloody hell! I was determined to carry on, however, and on race day to run the entire marathon distance. As the weeks went by, drawing ever closer to the big event, the training became easier and I was indeed losing quite a lot of weight. I had to admit I was really enjoying myself, and I felt much better than I had done for a long time. I did run the marathon, completing it in 3 hours 40 minutes, running all the way!

As the time progressed, my enthusiasm varied: some years I did lots of training, other years I did only enough to keep my fitness and weight from regressing. I always had a feeling of wanting to do better, to beat my previous personal best and, to date, after participating in 54 half marathons and nine full marathons, my personal best for each event stands at 1 hour 19 minutes for the former and 2 hours 57 minutes for the latter.

As I trained, I became increasingly bored with the same old city streets, looking constantly for new routes to run. I also became more and more aware of the difficulty (from both points of view) of sharing the streets with traffic. With both runners and motorists trying to get to where they want to go as fast as they can – with neither prepared to give way to the other – it is a particularly dangerous situation for the runner, as I have found almost to my cost on several occasions. In an effort to get off the roads altogether, I started to use the long-distance footpaths, canal towpaths and cycleways which, in the case of the canal, had been in existence for a long time. Others have recently been upgraded to suit today's environmental needs.

The more I explored these tracks, the more I began to realise that it was almost possible to traverse Glasgow in all directions without using the city streets at all. Only occasionally was it necessary even to have to cross a street. I found that these city routes continued for great distances into the countryside, and that there are many rights-of-way all around central Scotland.

In many cases information on these facilities is plentiful, particularly the cycleways, and there are many brochures already available. The canal also has had many pamphlets written on all aspects of the leisure activities available to the public. It is not my intention to undermine any of these excellent publications, but rather to supplement this information and to cover new ground.

In this book I have tried to show the way these various tracks throughout central Scotland link together to form a network stretching in every direction. It enables the reader to make his or her way through or around Glasgow in all directions without contact with traffic, and also to get from within the city – and many other towns in the area – to deep into the countryside without having to use any form of vehicular transport.

Although the greatest emphasis must be on leisure, there is another very important dimension which I should bring to the reader's attention: that is, to be able to use parts of this network of tracks to commute to work using self-motivating transportation – walking, running or cycling. In Glasgow, for instance, it is possible to travel in this way into the centre from outlying areas on all sides of the city. In other districts there are also such links, for instance in East Kilbride, Loudoun, Renfrew, Monklands, Motherwell, Hamilton, Clydesdale, Strathkelvin, Cumbernauld and Kilsyth, Stirling and many more throughout Central Scotland. It is possible, for example, to cycle faster from either Bearsden or Milngavie into the centre of Glasgow in the rush hour than it is to drive, and this can be done in the peace of an off-road track.

Throughout the area there is an abundance of such tracks which few of us know about, far less make use of, allowing the user to cover great or small distances in peace and quiet. Even in the middle of Glasgow, there are areas of great scenic beauty, some of which are only a stone's throw from the hustle and bustle of the city centre. It is possible, for instance, to travel from the south-east of the city across to the north-west and beyond, along the banks of two of Glasgow's rivers, the Clyde and the Kelvin, a distance of some 16 miles all within the boundaries of the city, only sharing the route with traffic for less than a quarter of a mile.

More and more of these routes are being developed by local authorities; indeed, plans are already being drawn up to link two of Scotland's most famous long-distance footpaths (the Southern Upland Way and the West Highland Way), a distance, when complete, of approximately 275 miles of continuous footpath

19

through some of the most spectacular scenery in the country. The existing route along Glasgow's river-banks will form part of the link between these two footpaths.

Within this network many tracks have already been upgraded to a high standard by the various local authorities (in conjunction with Sustrans in the case of cycle tracks). There are many more, however, which exist in a less formal state and although they cannot be said to have a consistent surface they are nevertheless serviceable and form an intrinsic part of the network. Some of these tracks are scheduled for upgrading in the future. By bringing these tracks to the attention of the reader in the form of a continuous network which can be used in many ways – for long distances or short, for business or pleasure – I would hope that the added interest engendered would make local authorities more aware of the importance of these tracks as an alternative to roads and road transport, and therefore bring their upgrading higher up the list of priorities.

As well as tracks, I have also pointed out disused railway lines, most of which are still owned by British Rail, and unclassified roads less than 4m wide which tend to have a very small amount of vehicular traffic on them and which are therefore extremely well suited for walking, running or cycling. In this time of ever-greater environmental threats to the planet, anything that can be done to reduce pollution in any way at all should surely be encouraged.

All of the routes I have written about in this book are on public land but there are small areas contained within some of the routes which, in order to avoid large detours, have had to cross very small stretches of private land. In these areas I personally found no problems when crossing and I never encountered, in any area, a sign prohibiting the public from crossing this land. However, I would like to point out that there is a law of trespass in Scotland, and although one cannot be prosecuted for crossing public land, it is possible to be sued for damage and to be asked to leave. I would therefore offer the following guidelines:

(1) If you come across a sign prohibiting you from a stretch of land, respect this and find an alternative route.

(2) If you are about to enter private land knowingly, try, if feasible, to gain the owner's permission before doing so.

(3) If challenged (unless you are completely sure the land you are walking on is public or is a right-of-way), leave the private land by the shortest available route.

(4) Whether private or public land, do not cause a nuisance in any way. Do not cause damage to crops, property or fences. Close all gates and do not frighten farm animals.

(5) Keep dogs under control at all times.

If these common-sense rules are applied, no one can have any justifiable grievance with you.

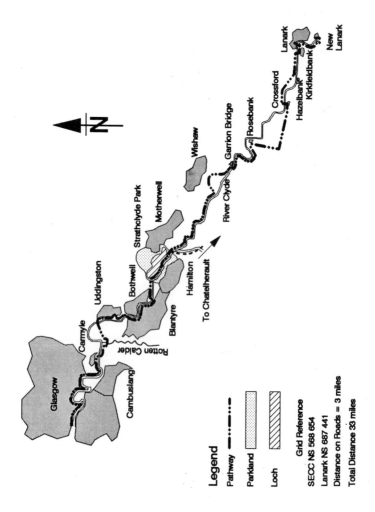

N

Legend

Pathway
Parkland
Loch

Grid Reference
SECC NS 568 654
Lanark NS 687 441
Distance on Roads = 3 miles
Total Distance 33 miles

Glasgow
Cambuslang
Carmyle
Rotten Calder
Uddingston
Bothwell
Blantyre
Strathclyde Park
Motherwell
Hamilton
To Chatelherault
Wishaw
River Clyde
Garrion Bridge
Rosebank
Crossford
Hazelbank
Kirkfieldbank
Lanark
New Lanark

CHAPTER 1

The Clyde Walkway

The Clyde Walkway starts at the west end of the carpark of the Scottish Exhibition and Conference Centre where it joins the Glasgow to Loch Lomond and Killin Cycleway heading west, and the Kelvin Walkway heading north-west at the footbridge over the Clydeside Expressway. It heads east along the riverside past the Moathouse Hotel and past Bell's Bridge. This is the link across the Clyde for pedestrians and cyclists travelling between the walkways and cycleways in the north to the Glasgow to Irvine Cycleway and other walkways on the south side of the river.

This area was once the site of two great docks: Queen's Dock on the north bank and Prince's Dock on the south. Both were closed in the early 1970s owing to the dwindling amount of shipping using them. Until the early 1960s, however, this whole area of the Clyde would have been crowded with ships from all over the world, loading and unloading everything under the sun. Queen's Dock was filled in prior to the construction of the SECC which was opened in 1985. Later Prince's Dock was filled in as a huge land renewal project and was used as the site of the very successful 1988 Scottish International Garden Festival. Many Glaswegians felt the Festival's six-month duration was far too short, and much of the site has lain derelict since that time despite assurances from certain quarters that this would not happen.

Here can also be seen the Finnieston Crane, the largest on the Clyde, which stands over 100ft high and has a maximum load of 160 tonnes. It was built in 1932 and is still fully operational today – and indeed must always remain so, for as well as being used to lift very heavy loads on a commercial basis, it also has military uses. Until the demise of the North British Locomotive Works in Springburn, this crane was used extensively to lift locomotives on to ships for export to countries such as India, South Africa, China and the United States of America. In fact, at one time Springburn supplied a quarter of all the world's locomotives. One of Springburn's locomotives which was used by South African Railways is once again back in Scotland, and can be seen at the Summerlee Heritage Centre in Coatbridge.

Directly across the Broomielaw from the Finnieston Crane can be seen one of two Rotundas. Now a restaurant and bar complex, this building was the northern entrance of the Finnieston Harbour Tunnel under the Clyde. The tunnel, which opened in 1896, was constructed with three separate tunnels, two for horse-drawn vehicles going in either direction, and one for pedestrians. Within the Rotunda building was housed the mechanism for six hydraulic lifts which took the vehicles from street level down to the tunnel floor, as well as a set of stairs for pedestrians. The tunnel lay derelict for years with its entrances securely blocked off, until it was proposed as a means of access from the north side of the city to the Garden Festival. When Strathclyde Regional Council Roads Department surveyed it, however, it was found to be in a dangerous condition, so the tunnels were sealed up and flooded. Bell's Bridge was then constructed to give access from the north side of the city.

Onwards to Anderston Quay, where the paddle-steamer *Waverley* is berthed when in Glasgow. This is the only paddle-steamer left in the British Isles and, when she is not taking passengers 'doon the watter', travels great distances to many ports in England to provide more people with the opportunity of a sail and a taste of her magic. Continue further on, under the Kingston Bridge which carries the M8 motorway high above the city streets. Now within the city centre, the way continues past King George V Bridge, Glasgow Bridge, the Suspension Bridge, Victoria Bridge and Albert Bridge – the five fine bridges across the Clyde. They look outstanding at night when floodlit against the darkened sky. The Victoria Bridge is on the site of the city's first bridge across the Clyde – the Glasgow Bridge. This is now the heart of the ancient city of Glasgow. The name Glasgow is accepted as coming from the Gaelic, *Glas* meaning 'green' and *ghu* meaning 'dear': dear green place. St Mungo, Glasgow's patron saint, founded a settlement on the banks of the Clyde in 543AD, and established a church on the hill above the settlement. This was to become Glasgow Cathedral.

The Saltmarket runs north from Albert Bridge to Glasgow Cross, High Street and Castle Street, and among the places of historical interest that can be found here are the High Court, Glasgow Green, the Tolbooth, Provand's Lordship (the oldest house in Glasgow, built by Bishop Andrew Muirhead in 1471) and Glasgow Cathedral. Parts of the latter date from the twelfth century, and St Mungo's tomb is in the crypt.

This is also the area where many of the city's markets were situated. For instance, the imposing building opposite Victoria Bridge is the Briggait. This building was the former fish market, built in 1873 in the French classical style, and the steeple that can be seen is part of the old Merchant House which stood on the site previously. As well as the official markets, there were also the unofficial ones, Paddy's Market being an example of the latter which has survived until the present day. It is situated between the Briggait and the High Court, and was so named because in the 1840s many famine-stricken Irish immigrants sold their clothes there to get money to feed their families.

The walkway enters Glasgow Green at Saltmarket and Jail Square. Glasgow Green, now a park, has been a civic amenity for 800 years and, as the name suggests, was used as a public drying green in the eighteenth and nineteenth centuries. It also served as the first location of the Glasgow Golf Club, which was established there in the eighteenth century. The Glasgow Fair was also located on the Green for generations. In the later part of the nineteenth century, the city's two major football clubs were founded there, Rangers in 1873 and Celtic in 1888. More recently, Glasgow Green has been used as the starting and finishing point of the Glasgow Marathon and the Great Scottish Run (a half marathon).

The Green is also the home of the People's Palace, one of Glasgow's finest museums, which houses a permanent exhibition of the city's history. Attached to the museum is a beautiful winter garden. The People's Palace was opened by Lord Rosebery on 22 January 1898, one of many 'people's palaces' to be opened in various parts of the world around this time. The idea behind this was that ordinary people should be given the opportunity to enjoy the pleasures purchased by the rich, such as music, art, singing and dancing. Not all of these museums developed in the same way, however; the one which was built in the East End of London, for instance, concentrated more on education, and ultimately became a polytechnic which is now part of the University of London.

Glasgow Green is the site of a 143ft-high monument built in 1806 to commemorate the great victories of Lord Nelson, and was the first such monument to be erected in Britain. On the city side of the Green is Templeton's Carpet Factory, a large and very ornate building. When James Templeton sought planning permission to build a factory in the immediate vicinity of Glasgow Green, the City Fathers refused to grant permission for a common factory to be built here and insisted that he erect a building which would enhance the area, so Templeton's architect, William Leaper, modelled the building on the Doge's Palace in Venice. This fine brick building, completed in 1889, closed as a carpet factory in 1979, but re-opened later as a business centre.

The way continues under King's Bridge and alongside Fleshers' Haugh, land which was purchased by the city in 1792 and incorporated into the Green. This is where Charles Edward Stuart, the Young Pretender, reviewed his troops in January 1746 after their long march north. The Jacobite army under the

Prince's lieutenant-general, Lord George Murray, occupied Glasgow for ten days, but as with the other Lowland areas they had passed through on their way north, they found the Glasgow people hostile. Indeed, it is said that the city magistrates had to be compelled to supply the army with new clothes so that the review could take place. Today Fleshers' Haugh is where the city holds its annual firework display on Guy Fawkes' night.

The route leaves Glasgow Green and goes under Shawfield Road at Rutherglen Bridge, following the Clyde as it meanders through the District of Dalmarnock, under Dalmarnock Bridge and on into Carmyle. The path, which up until now has been wide and formal, becomes much rougher at this point but is in no way difficult. Carry on to a disused railway viaduct which runs high over the Clyde. It is a bit of a scramble to get to the top of the viaduct but this is not particularly arduous. Once at the top, cross the river and take the path down the other side, back to the river's edge. The path roughly follows the river-bank for about a mile or so until it comes to a small river known as the Rotten Calder. Here the path turns south, away from the River Clyde. Follow this river for just under a quarter of a mile to where a footbridge spans the burn. The path broadens out here and, after going under the main railway line to the south, climbs steadily to the B758, known locally as the Blantyre Farm road. Turn right here and walk up this road for some 50m to where the path commences again on the opposite side of the road. From here on, the path is well defined and easy to follow.

After about half a mile the path has once again made its way back down to the river, to where there is a footbridge to take the walker across the river and into Uddingston. The name Uddingston or Odistoun means 'Oda's Farm'. Once the river has been crossed, turn right. Within the next quarter of a mile or so the traveller will come across many junctions on the path – local access points – which are not signposted. Every time a junction is reached, the traveller should go to the right, thus ensuring that the correct route is followed.

Still clearly defined, the path continues through a pleasant wooded area with the river meandering alongside. The route

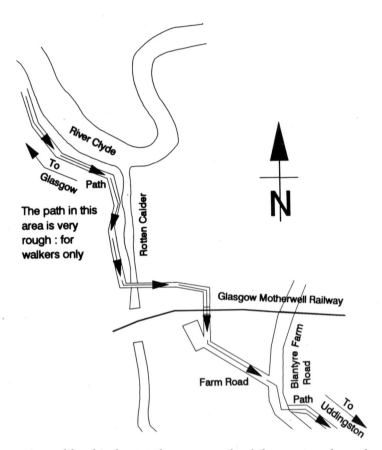

continues like this for a mile or so until, whilst turning through a bend in the river, the path climbs to the top of a gorge, to where a gate is reached. Once through the gate the traveller immediately comes upon the ancient red sandstone façade of Bothwell Castle. The name Bothwell comes from 'St Bathan's well', St Bathan being the Abbot of Bangor in the mid-seventh century.

Bothwell Castle has a very important place in Scottish history. The castle itself dates from the later part of the thirteenth century and was built by Walter de Moravia (or Moray). The oldest part of the castle is the great circular tower or donjon (*donjon* being a French word meaning 'keep' or 'stronghold' and from this comes our English word 'dungeon'). Bothwell Castle was an extremely strong fortification and when it was attacked by the English King Edward I in 1301, during the Scottish Wars of Independence, it was only taken by deploying a massive siege engine. After the Battle of Bannockburn in 1314 the castle was surrendered to the Scots, who partially dismantled it. Retaken by Edward III in 1336, the castle was won back for Scotland in 1337 by Sir Andrew de Moray, who then partly demolished the donjon. It was then acquired in 1362 by Archibald the Grim, the third Earl of Douglas, who went about rebuilding the castle. This rebuilding went on through several generations of the Douglas family, and the castle as it stands today was finished around 1500. It was acquired in 1669 by another Archibald Douglas, the first Earl of Forfar, who demolished part of it, using the castle stone to build a mansion now itself demolished. Since that time the castle has remained as we see it today. It was taken over by the state as an historical monument in 1935, and is worth many hours of exploration.

The path, which goes through the castle grounds in front of the south façade and leaves again by a gate, winds its way back to

Bothwell Castle from the Clyde Walkway

29

the riverside. Here there is a sign erected by the Clyde Calders Project which states: 'This is the end of The Clyde Walkway. Private property beyond this point.' If, however, the traveller carries on some 10m further along the path – which he or she has a legal right to do – as the path turns a corner, a set of steps which climb up through the steep, wooded hillside away from the river can be seen. This is the legal route avoiding the private land and involves no more than a 15-minute detour.

Take the steps to the top of the hill and carry on to a junction in the path; turn left here, climb three or four more steps, and continue on to the junction with a road. At this road, turn left and continue for some 100m to the road junction with Castle Avenue. Turn right here and follow this road for about 250m or so; the path recommences on the right and, within a short distance, winds back down to the riverside by another set of steps to continue as before.

A little further on, the path comes out on to Blantyre Mill Road. Cross the footbridge to the other side of the Clyde to where the David Livingstone Memorial Centre is located. The focal point of the centre is the 'single-end' – a one-room apartment – in the eighteenth-century tenement block where the

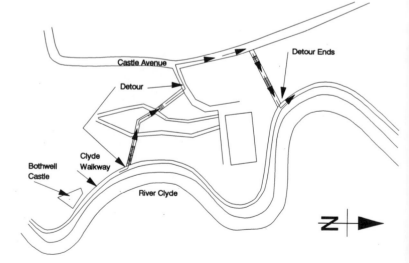

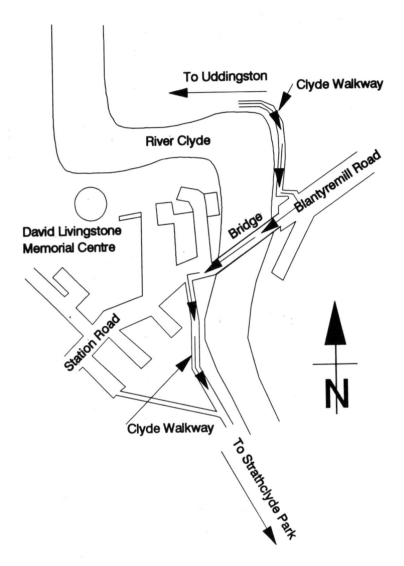

famous Scottish explorer was born in 1813. This building, which once housed 24 families, is now a museum devoted to Livingstone's life and work. Within the grounds are also located the African Pavilion, an adventure playground, tea-room and shop, and is worth a full day's visit.

31

Across from the Centre the path continues. Back once more on the south bank of the river, the still clearly defined path takes a route along the top of a much higher and steeper bank. Soon after joining the route at Blantyre, the path dips into a gorge. Climbing up the other side by way of some steps, a junction is reached on the left halfway up these steps. Follow this path to the left to a clearing and here take the first path on the left. Within a mile the path joins a disused railway. The supports of the high railway viaduct can still be seen jutting out of the river, although the bridge superstructure has been demolished. Follow this railway away from the river to where a road can be seen. Turn left on to this road and follow it round past the entrance to Craighead Retreat House. Here it joins the segregated footpath which runs parallel to the A725, the East Kilbride Expressway. This footpath sweeps down a long hill to where it joins the B7071 Bothwell to Hamilton road at Bothwell Bridge. The route from the dismantled railway to Bothwell Bridge is temporary, and will eventually carry straight on along the river-bank to Bothwell Bridge; it should be finished in the not too distant future.

Bothwell Brig is the site of the famous battle of the same name where, in 1679, a force of 4,000 Covenanters were heavily defeated by an army sent by the Government under the leadership of James, Duke of Monmouth, the illegitimate son of King Charles II. Some 400 Covenanters were killed and 1,200 were taken prisoner. The prisoners were sent to Edinburgh and herded into Greyfriars churchyard to await their eventual execution, imprisonment or deportation.

Next to the monument commemorating the battle, the path leaves the road and follows the river for a short distance before it sweeps round past an area of wetland. This is a very important bird sanctuary and has a wide variety of water-fowl and many other species of birds including the Smew – the sanctuary is possibly the only place in Scotland where this bird can be found.

From here, cross the exit and entry slip roads of the M74 which link with the roundabout on the A725. At the next opening after the motorway's southbound entry slip road, enter Strathclyde Park and follow the signpost for the Visitor Centre (Chapter 5 gives a fuller description of the park's facilities). On reaching the Visitor Centre, take the footpath along the south-western shore of Strathclyde Loch. The loch is over a mile in length; three-quarters of the way along it a footpath goes off to the right, over the River Clyde which runs parallel to Strathclyde Loch, through a walkway under the motorway, and out on to the Hamilton side at the mausoleum.

Hamilton Mausoleum, with its magnificent domed roof, was commissioned in 1841 by Alexander, the tenth Duke of Hamilton, who was nicknamed 'Il Magnifico'. The building's principal architect, David Bryce, took 16 years to build it. It is a copy of the Castel Sant'Angelo in Rome – the Emperor Hadrian's mausoleum – and the doors are a copy of those in the Baptistry in Florence. This was to be the family burial place and have a chapel above, but a terrible echo made the latter impossible. Alexander had all his ancestors exhumed and re-interred in the crypt of the mausoleum in 1852, he himself being laid to rest in the chapel later that same year.

After passing the mausoleum, the path enters Hamilton not far from the town centre. The route to Lanark leaves Strathclyde Park by way of the Spine Road, as the road through the park is known, where it joins the A723. Cross the A723 at the pedestrian crossing at Airbles Road. Walk along this road for some 50m to where a path can be seen skirting a housing estate. Follow this path as far as it goes, until the route along the river begins on the right. The path is broad and well maintained for the next two miles and the terrain varies between woodland and open country-side and is very pleasant. Beyond this, the path becomes narrow but is still an easy walk, until the route is barred by a pumping station right on the banks of the river. There is a very rough path around the pumping station but at the other side, as it rejoins the river-bank, the path is not a right-of-way and therefore should not be used. The right-of-way is via the access road from the pumping station to Muirhouse, and then east to Dalzell Country Park and past Dalzell House. Once past this, the road winds back to the river-bank and continues for some three miles or so.

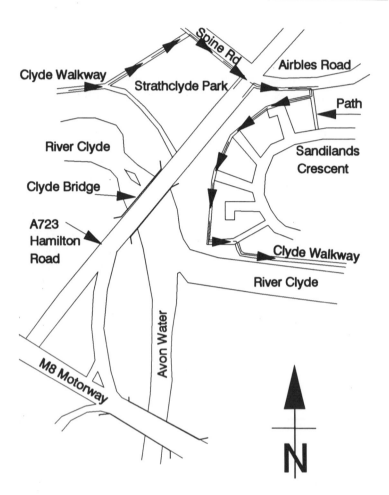

To the north-east of the river can be seen Cambusnethan Priory, which was built as a private house for Robert Lockhart of Castlehill in 1819; the 'Priory' tag is an affectation, as it has never been a religious house. Although this building looks imposing from a distance, it is in fact a burnt-out shell in a most dangerous condition.

About a quarter of a mile past the place on the river-bank approximately level with Cambusnethan, the right-of-way heads inland, joining a small unmade road known as the Garrionhaugh road. Turn right on to this road and follow it to where it joins the A71 opposite the junction of the B7011 Brownlee and Law Road just north of Garrion Bridge.

Between Garrion Bridge and Kirkfieldbank the footpath along the river-bank peters out. There is a footpath on the road from Brownlee to Carluke which heads down to the river at Milton-Lochart and over the Clyde at the access bridge at Overton. Milton-Lochart House, which was once bought by Sir Walter Scott for his son-in-law, was recently taken down stone by stone and shipped off to Japan to become the centrepiece of a children's fantasy theme park.

Close by, at Milton Head, is the birthplace of Major-General William Roy of the Royal Engineers. Born in 1726, he is best known for preparing the map of mainland Scotland known as the Duke of Cumberland's Map which is now in the British Museum in London. He is also known for his work on the subject of the Roman occupation of Britain.

There are two alternative routes which could be followed from the end of Garrionhaugh Road. The first is to carry on to Garrion Bridge and simply walk along the A72 to Kirkfieldbank, going through Rosebank where there is a right-of-way for some

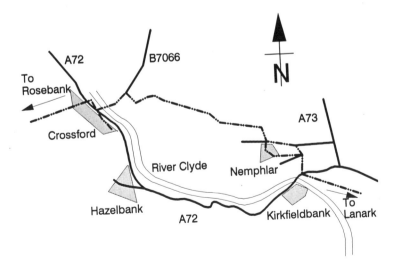

distance along the banks of the Clyde. When this ends, the route goes back to the road as it passes through Crossford and Hazelbank to Kirkfieldbank. Although along a fairly busy road, this is not an unpleasant walk since it passes through the heart of one of Scotland's more abundant fruit-growing areas.

The alternative is to walk as before along the A72 to Rosebank, where a right-of-way is indicated by a signpost on the opposite side of the road from the river. Take this as it ascends the hill. About half a mile on, it converges with a minor road. Turn right on to this road and follow it for about a quarter of a mile to the start of a right-of-way which descends a long hill down to Crossford. From Crossford take the B7066 Braidwood Road across the Clyde and then the minor road to Nemphlar and on to Kirkfieldbank. This is the way I would recommend, as it keeps walking on major roads to an absolute minimum.

From Kirkfieldbank the path to Lanark restarts. From the south side of the bridge over the Clyde, take the road to the right where it passes a house and continue downhill to the path, which then climbs steadily for over half a mile to Castlebank Park in the town of Lanark.

Lanark, which means 'long glade', is a medieval town of some importance. It is said that it became a burgh as early as 1140, although there is little evidence to substantiate this claim. Other important events did take place here, however: the Scottish parliament was convened in Lanark between 1293 and 1295; and William Wallace of Elderslie became a local hero in the town after he killed the English sheriff, Hazelrig, for allegedly being involved in the killing of Wallace's wife and the burning of his house in the Castlegate. News of Wallace's exploits inspired others, who flocked to join him in the fight against the English occupation. There is a statue of him on the front of St Nicholas' Church, facing the High Street, which was a gift to the town in 1822. Lanark today is a very pleasant market town well worth exploring.

From Kirkfieldbank there is also a path to New Lanark. Take the minor road towards Byretown, and in a very short distance the entrance to the West Lodge of the Corehouse Estate is

The Falls of Clyde

reached. This estate is a nature reserve managed by the Scottish Wildlife Trust. Within the estate the path goes all the way up to the weir at Bonnington Linn – the beginning of the Clyde gorge – and on down the other side of the river to New Lanark. At the weir some of the water is diverted into an aqueduct, where it runs with great force down to Bonnington Power Station to drive the turbines. The water which is not diverted through the aqueduct tumbles over steep cliffs and becomes a fast-flowing torrent, reaching Corra Linn a mile further on where it cascades in three stages almost 30m over steep rocks past the ruins of Corra Castle. This area is known as the Falls of Clyde and is a famous beauty spot.

Half a mile further on the river passes the town of New Lanark which was built by David Dale (1739–1806). Work started in 1785 after Dale had brought Richard Arkwright, the inventor of the water frame, to view the falls; the two men agreed that this was a plentiful source of cheap power and formed a partnership to build cotton-spining mills. The construction work was undertaken by Dale, while Arkwright trained people to build and operate spinning frames. Most of the labour came from pauper and orphan children living in the workhouses of Glasgow and Edinburgh, who were apprenticed as mill hands. David Dale found it impossible to recruit enough workers locally, however. His problem was solved in 1791: a ship-load of emigrants from the Highlands had set sail to America but their ship was damaged in a storm, and put back to port at Greenock; Dale offered the passengers work and housing in his new mill village. By 1795 a workforce of 1,500 was employed at the mills and lived in the specially constructed tenement blocks.

In 1800 Dale's son-in-law, Robert Owen, bought the mills from him for £60,000 and set about improving and expanding the business. Robert Owen introduced many social and educational reforms to improve the quality of life of his workers and their families. He phased out the use of child labour and introduced schooling, including the first nursery school in the world. The village store was run for the benefit of the community. By bulk buying, the profits met some of the running costs of the school.

New Lanark Mills

This was considered to be the forerunner of the Co-operative movement.

Today New Lanark is a living museum of its time. Many of the tenement houses are once again occupied and more blocks are being refurbished all the time. Within the visitor centre in the institute and in Mill 3, one is able to take a trip back in time into New Lanark's past in a very special history tour called The Annie McLeod Experience. There are also exhibition areas and good catering facilities within the visitor centre.

The path or series of paths in this chapter are very varied in their state and condition. In some places they have been upgraded and are broad with a good surface, while other parts are very rough. The route described is not particularly strenuous, apart from the fact that it is 37 miles long; if it is tackled in one go, it is, of course, a very long walk. It *is* a walk, because many parts of the route are impassable by bicycle. It is worth noting, however, that the Planning Departments of Glasgow, Hamilton, Motherwell and Nithsdale District Councils are all at various stages of planning the development of this walkway; the intention is that the path will be upgraded to become a formal long-distance footpath from Glasgow to Lanark, following the river wherever feasible. Some of this work has already been carried out, and in many areas the path is already in excellent condition.

CHAPTER 2

Walkway from Strathclyde Park to Strathaven via Chatelherault

On leaving Strathclyde Park at the south-eastern exit, climb the steps up to the A723 Hamilton-to-Motherwell road, walk across to the far side of the road and cross the Clyde Bridge towards Hamilton. A short distance after the bridge has been crossed there is a small stile at the fence by the side of the footpath – blink and you will miss it! Climb over this fence and continue down the embankment on the other side, and this will take you straight on to the path to Chatelherault.

The path turns to run alongside the south bank of the River Clyde just before the spot where the River Avon flows into it. From there it follows the Avon upstream, passing under the massive bridge which carries the M8 motorway high above. It then passes Haughead where a small stream is crossed by way of a footbridge. Continue on under the A72 at Ferniegair and over the Old Avon Bridge, to where the entrance to Chatelherault Country Park is situated.

The park is well signposted and contains many places of interest. Chatelherault was a hunting lodge commissioned by James, the fifth Duke of Hamilton. The beautiful building was designed by William Adam and was completed in 1744. At the

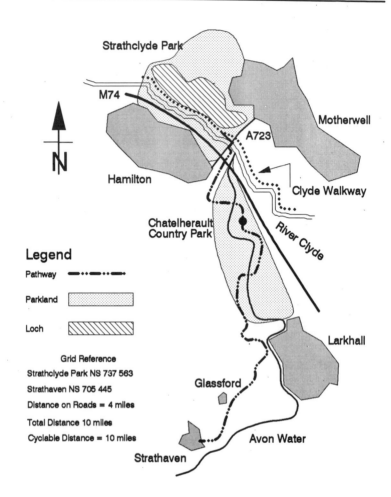

time of its completion there was a huge swathe of wide parkland bordered by trees which linked Chatelherault with Hamilton Palace in the valley below. This was known as the grand avenue, and parts of it can still be seen today as the trees have been replanted. As the town of Hamilton itself has increased in size, much of this land has been built upon and, of course, Hamilton Palace no longer exists, having been demolished in 1922 due to subsidence. This subsidence was caused by the twelfth Duke who, in order to finance his insatiable gambling habit, allowed more

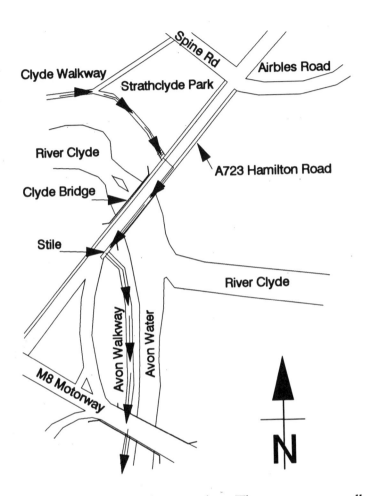

seams in his coalmines to be opened up. These seams eventually undermined the palace foundations.

The derelict Chatelherault was acquired for the nation in 1968. Restoration commenced in 1979 and the park was opened in 1986. There is also a visitor centre in the William Adam Lodge, which has an audio-visual presentation of the history of Chatel-herault. There is also a tableau of wax figures representing characters who lived and worked on the estate in the eighteenth century. Near these fine buildings is a garden centre and cafeteria.

43

Within the park itself there are many walks, most of which are described in leaflets available at the visitor centre. These walks are signposted along their routes and it is possible to spend many hours exploring the area. On the way the reader will see the site of an iron-age fort, the ruined Cadzow Castle (which, unfortunately, is too dangerous to explore and has been cordoned off), the Cadzow Oaks, which were planted in the fifteenth century, the herd of Cadzow cattle descended from the original herd which would have roamed freely in the forest, and the 80ft-high Duke's Bridge over the Avon.

On now to Strathaven. Wherever you are in Chatelherault the paths are all well signposted, so now follow the directions for the 'White Bridge', which was constructed originally for the miners. Cross this bridge and carry on up to the top of the hill. Turn left here and follow the path as it runs parallel to the River Avon, now flowing far below. Take the second opening on the right which should be signposted 'Footpath to Millheugh'.

An alternative route (especially for cyclists) is to go via the 'Green Bridge', after which take the path to the top of the hill and there join the footpath to Millheugh. Carry on to a crossroads, go straight across and, following the unclassified road for about a mile and a half, pass under a dismantled railway to a road junction at Low Kittymuir Farm (there are plans to open this line again as far as Stonehouse and from there on it has been used as the line of the new Stonehouse Bypass). Here turn left to Crofthead (there may be a sign at this junction indicating the road is closed half a mile ahead, but ignore this because the walk route turns off this road within quarter of a mile); turn right again and follow this road all the way to Glassford. Once you have reached Glassford follow the signs for Strathaven, which is just over a mile from there.

An alternative route, which avoids the last mile on the Glassford-Strathaven road (sometimes this road, although minor, can be busy) is as follows: at the first junction on this stretch of road turn left (it is signposted for Stonehouse) and at a fork in the road go right to Glassford Bridge. Before crossing the bridge, turn right on to a right-of-way known as the 'Old Coach Road'.

Duke's Bridge in Chatelherault Country Park

This is by way of a stile and for the first few hundred metres the path is a bit of a scramble; it soon opens out once again to a narrow track road which finishes at the edge of Strathaven on the Glassford road, only a stone's-throw from the heart of the town.

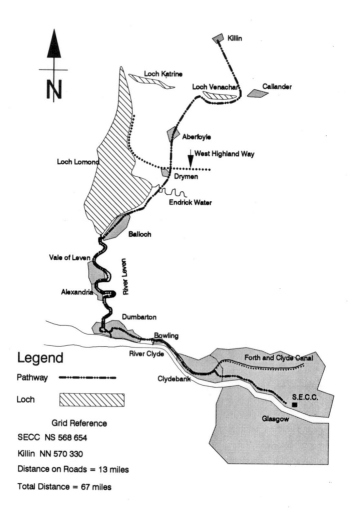

N

Killin

Loch Katrine

Loch Venachar   Callander

Aberfoyle

West Highland Way

Loch Lomond   Drymen

Endrick Water

Balloch

Vale of Leven   River Leven

Alexandria

Dumbarton

Bowling

River Clyde   Forth and Clyde Canal

Legend

Pathway   ▰▰▰▰▰▰

Loch   ▨▨▨▨

Clydebank

S.E.C.C.

Glasgow

Grid Reference

SECC NS 568 654

Killin NN 570 330

Distance on Roads = 13 miles

Total Distance = 67 miles

CHAPTER 3

The Glasgow, Loch Lomond and Killin Cycleway

The Glasgow to Loch Lomond Cycleway is well documented, its route described in a widely available brochure published by the various district councils within whose area it passes. Therefore, as with the West Highland Way, I don't intend to describe this route in detail, and will only refer to it as a means of getting to or joining up with other walkways or rights-of-way which are perhaps not as well known.

The Glasgow-Loch Lomond Cycleway starts where the Clyde Walkway finishes. Cross the footbridge which spans the Clydeside Expressway and turn along the footpath by the side of the Expressway in a westerly direction. The route is well signposted, and not far after Partick railway station, the way joins the line of the old Lanarkshire and Dumbartonshire Railway where it stays until it joins the Forth and Clyde Canal at Clydebank. The route along the canal is described in Chapter 5.

This then brings the cycleway to Bowling and from here it is only four miles to Dumbarton. Just before arriving in Dumbarton the traveller passes Milton. Here, adjacent to the cycle track at the rear of a petrol station, the management have

47

provided tables and chairs for the enjoyment of some refreshment – from the garage shop, of course. There are also toilet facilities here. Just across the garage forecourt and the main road is a road called Milton Brae which leads directly into the Kilpatrick Hills where there are many fine hill walks. It is possible, for instance, to get from there to the Whangie and Queen's View and on as far as Drymen Road.

Dumbarton (so called by the Angles – *dun* meaning 'rock' or 'fort' and *briton* being changed to 'barton' – 'the fort of the Britons') is the ancient capital of the Celtic kingdom of Strathclyde. Since the end of the Roman occupation in about 430AD, the southern part of the British Isles was overrun by barbaric invaders from across the North Sea, the Angles and Saxons, who pushed the native Britons westwards into Wales and Cornwall and north into Cumbria and Strathclyde. In Strathclyde the first of these Celtic tribes was the Regnum Cambrensi. They spoke a language very similar to Welsh, and named Glasgow's river the Clyde. Strathclyde is also known as one of the places which King Arthur once ruled. There are many references to *Castri Arthuri*, one of these being made by David II, King of Scots, in his parliamentary records.

The Britons ruled over Strathclyde till 1018 when the last King of the Britons died without an heir, and was succeeded by Duncan, the grandson of Malcolm II, King of Scots, and the heir to the Scottish throne. Sixteen years later Malcolm II died and Duncan succeeded him, and for the first time all Scotland was under one rule.

There is no other place in Scotland that has had a longer recorded history as a stronghold than the castle on Dumbarton Rock. Built on an extinct volcano, it was seen in the Middle Ages as well-nigh impregnable: 'a castell stronge and harde for to obteine'. William Wallace was held there for a time, before he was sent to London for trial and execution. Mary Queen of Scots lived in the castle for a time as a child, and it was from there she was sent to France to marry the young Dauphin. Later in her reign, after her defeat at the Battle of Langside and her flight to England, the castle was defended for her by Lord Fleming, the

Governor, until it was finally taken by Captain Crawfurd of Jordanhill in 1571. Although thought to be impregnable, the Earl of Lennox (on whose land the castle was) heard that there was in fact a way up the castle rock, so he sent 200 men commanded by Captain Crawfurd to take it. Crawfurd and his men arrived at the foot of the castle rock around two o'clock in the morning, laden with ladders, ropes, and long poles with hooks, and began clambering up the steep rocks on the north side of the eastern peak. It was dawn by the time Crawfurd's men climbed the wall at the summit of the rock and, in the early morning mist, they charged down to the garrison below. The garrison was taken swiftly in this surprise attack with only three men killed, and all the rest taken prisoner. Lord Fleming managed to escape by scrambling down steep rocks to a postern gate and into a small boat moored on the Clyde. He made his way first to Argyll and then to France. His wife, the French Ambassador and the Archbishop of St Andrews were not so lucky; they were all taken prisoner and the Archbishop later executed. For his great efforts Crawfurd was awarded a pension of £200 per annum to be paid from the revenues of St Andrews priory. The castle that is seen today dates from 1735, and was built by the English army to house the military governor.

The famous clipper, the *Cutty Sark*, was built in Dumbarton in 1869 at both the Scott Linton yard and William Deny's yard. The ship's name comes from Robert Burns's poem *Tam o' Shanter* and refers to the clothes worn by the witch who took Tam's fancy. The *Cutty Sark* plied between Shanghai and London with cargoes of tea, and later sailed as a wool clipper from Australia. She was still in service after the First World War, but is now moored at Greenwich in London.

After crossing the River Leven at Bridge Street, Dumbarton, and going under the Glasgow road, the way goes on along the banks of the Leven to Balloch and the southern extremity of Loch Lomond at Balloch Park. From Balloch the route follows a quiet back road surrounded by pleasant rolling countryside to the village of Croftamie, and on to Drymen via the main road for a short distance. Here the cycleway crosses the West Highland

Way as it heads towards the eastern end of Loch Lomond at Balmaha. Beyond Drymen the route again follows back roads before turning along forest tracks through the Loch Ard Forest – part of the Queen Elizabeth Forest Park – and on to Aberfoyle.

From this point on, the routes for cyclists are many and varied. More information about them can be obtained from the brochures produced by Sustrans. They are available from tourist boards throughout the country or from Sustrans office at 53 Cochrane Street, Glasgow G1 1HL. Sustrans is a charity and any donation, however small, is always welcome.

CHAPTER 4

The Kelvin Walkway

The Kelvin Walkway starts where the Clyde Walkway finishes. Just cross the footbridge which spans the Clydeside Expressway, turn along Sandyford Street for 200m into Yorkhill Park, out on to Old Dumbarton Road and left on to Bunhouse Road, running alongside the Kelvin Hall, Scotland's international indoor running track and sports complex. The Kelvin Hall (which also houses the Museum of Transport) was the second building to hold that name: the original building was destroyed by fire in July 1925 and the present building was opened by King George V two years later in July 1927. Its primary function, until it was superseded by SECC in 1986, was as an exhibition centre. In 1986 renovations began to change the building to suit its present function. The Museum of Transport was transferred from Coplawhill Tramway Works (now the Tramway Theatre) in Albert Drive in the South Side of the city and is an extremely interesting place, with new exhibits being put on display all the time. It is well worth a visit just to see the many examples of Glasgow's old tramcars which span all periods of their century-long reign as the city's primary form of public transport.

Across Dumbarton Road and into Kelvingrove Park, one

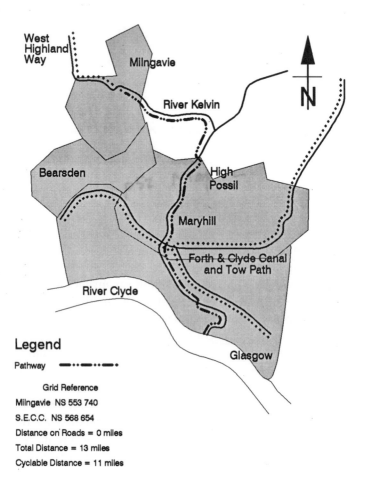

West
Highland
Way

Milngavie

River Kelvin

N

Bearsden

High
Possil

Maryhill

Forth & Clyde Canal
and Tow Path

River Clyde

Glasgow

Legend

Pathway ▬▪▬▪▪▬▪▬ ▪

Grid Reference

Milngavie NS 553 740

S.E.C.C. NS 568 654

Distance on Roads = 0 miles

Total Distance = 13 miles

Cyclable Distance = 11 miles

passes Glasgow University on the left on Gilmour Hill. The university moved here in 1870 from its original site in the High Street where it had been located since 1460, although the university had been in existence in the Chapterhouse and Lower Church of the Cathedral since 1451. It is Scotland's second-oldest university, after St Andrews. The university also houses the Hunterian Museum, where many of the relics of the Antonine Wall can be seen.

On the right is Kelvingrove Museum and Art Gallery which was built to coincide with Glasgow's second Great International Exhibition, that of 1901. Its fine collection of paintings includes works by Botticelli, Giorgione, Rembrandt, Millet, Monet, Van Gogh, Derain, Picasso and Dalí. This splendid building was purpose-built as an art gallery and museum and, after the Great Exhibition finished, was opened in its present form in 1902.

The place where the River Kelvin reaches the Clyde has great historical significance for Glasgow as it was the site of the city's flour mills from the sixteenth century. In 1568 permission was given for the first of these flour mills to be built by the Earl of Moray, Regent of Scotland, as a favour bestowed to the burghers of Glasgow for their great service to him at the Battle of Langside (where his forces defeated Mary Queen of Scots' army, led by the fifth Earl of Argyll). A succession of mills were built on this site, the last of which was still operating as late as the nineteenth century.

Once Kelvinway is crossed, an uninterrupted four-mile pathway begins along the banks of the river, passing under Kelvin Bridge which carries Great Western Road over the river. This is one of the many beautiful Victorian bridges which span the river along this stretch of the walkway. These bridges are carrying the busy city streets, for we are still in the heart of Glasgow. Where the walkway itself crosses the river a quarter of a mile further on, the remains of an old mill lade can still be seen. This is North Woodside Flint Mill which was still in operation until early this century.

Go on another quarter of a mile to a footbridge which crosses the river. This is one of the entrances to the Botanic Gardens, another of Glasgow's beautiful Victorian parks. One of the most important features of the Botanics is the Kibble Palace, which houses many species of tropical plants.

The walkway continues west towards Maryhill; on the right it passes some blocks of high flats which were built on the site of Maryhill Barracks, the home until 1959 of Glasgow's own regiment, the Highland Light Infantry.

The way continues across Kelvindale Road, passing under the aqueduct which carries the Forth and Clyde Canal above the Kelvin. If you want to transfer to the canal towpath here, there is a path which swings off to the right at the aqueduct. From here the walkway follows the line of the old Caledonian Railway yard which served local industry in the nineteenth and twentieth centuries until its decline.

The way leaves the banks of the Kelvin at Dalsholm Road, missing out on some very beautiful scenery. This is because there is no way through the Garscube Estate which now belongs to Glasgow University. The river runs through the estate for almost a mile and, for reasons best known to itself, the university wishes this land to remain very private indeed. This is very unfortunate, because apart from the fact that the house has been demolished, the estate is very much as it was in the nineteenth century.

From the river bridge at Dalsholm Road, turn left on to Maryhill Road, cross it and go into Maryhill Park, where the walkway joins the River Kelvin once again at Caldercuilt Road. By this time the city has been left behind, and the walkway meanders through the countryside following the Kelvin, passing the stables which are the Glasgow Headquarters for Riding for the Disabled, where the staff and a dedicated band of volunteers do a wonderful job.

On the other side of the river can be seen Killermont Estate, home of Glasgow's most exclusive golf club, where the men-only membership have to be asked to join, and even then only if they have been members of Glasgow Gailes.

After passing through a wooded area the way comes out on to an open stretch, and carries on along the top of an earth flood-dyke, until it comes to the point where, alas, it has to pass

Along the banks of the River Kelvin

alongside one of the biggest rubbish tips in Central Scotland. Oh, how it smells! Not even the attempts at landscaping can stop some very dubious liquids leaching through the ground at some points along this part of the route. If a timber bridge had been constructed over the river before the path reached this area, it would have been a vast improvement. This detraction is soon over, however, and is a small price to pay for a very beautiful and interesting walkway.

When Balmore Road is reached, the dump has been left behind and, after crossing the road, open countryside and fresh air return. Continue along the dyke until it reaches the place where the Allander Water flows into the Kelvin. There the path turns and carries on along the banks of the Allander becoming less formal for a time, until it reaches Balmore Road again. Once the road is crossed, the route to Milngavie is straightforward: cross Glasgow Road and enter Keystone Road, turn into Lennox Park and so reach Milngavie and the end of the walkway. In Milngavie the Kelvin Walkway joins the West Highland Way; the centre of the town is fully pedestrianised and the walkways are uninterrupted.

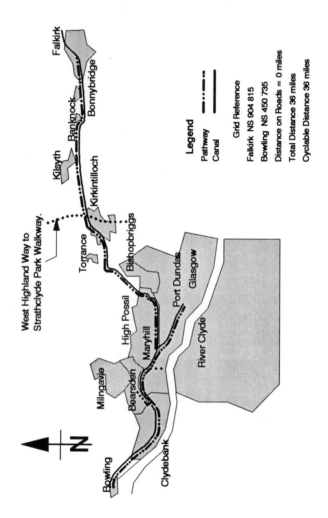

West Highland Way to Strathclyde Park Walkway.

N

Falkirk

Bonnybridge

Banknock

Kilsyth

Kirkintilloch

Torrance

Bishopbriggs

Port Dundas

Glasgow

High Possil

Maryhill

River Clyde

Milngavie

Bearsden

Clydebank

Bowling

Legend

Pathway ▪•••▪▪

Canal ─────

Grid Reference

Falkirk NS 904 815

Bowling NS 450 735

Distance on Roads = 0 miles

Total Distance 36 miles

Cyclable Distance 36 miles

CHAPTER 5

The Forth and Clyde Canal Towpath

The Forth and Clyde Canal passes through many areas which are steeped in history. It follows the same route as the Antonine Wall, which is the shortest distance between the east and west coasts of Scotland. Before the canal was built, ships wishing to sail from one side of the country to the other had to go round the north of Scotland, a very arduous and dangerous journey over 300 miles long. The proposed line of the canal, on the other hand, was only 35 miles long.

The engineer in charge of designing and constructing the canal was John Smeaton, who, some years before, had designed and built the Eddystone Lighthouse. Digging began at Grangemouth on the River Forth in 1768 and took 22 years to complete, finishing at Bowling on the River Clyde in 1790, where the company chairman poured a hogshead of Forth water into the Clyde.

The major part of the canal, from Grangemouth to Stockingfield where the main canal joins the Glasgow branch, was completed by 1775, but the Forth and Clyde Canal Company ran out of money and work stopped for ten years; within this time, however, the Glasgow branch was completed as far as

Hamiltonhill by an Act of Parliament. In 1791 this was extended, and Port Dundas was constructed together with the junction with the Monkland Canal. I intend to start with the Glasgow branch, from Port Dundas to Stockingfield, where this branch joins the main canal. I will then describe from there in a westerly direction, followed by the canal's course to the east.

Port Dundas is an area just north of the city centre. Until the 1950s it was the junction with the Monkland Canal at the Monklands Basin which has now been filled in, forming the line of the M8 motorway as far as Easterhouse.

As its name suggests, Port Dundas was built as a port. It took its name from the first governor of the Canal Company, Sir Thomas Dundas. It was built at One-Hundred-Acre-Hill, situated at the time above the city of Glasgow. Wharves, basins, granaries and warehouses were constructed. It also had a customs house, a toll-collector's house, and a bridge-keeper's house.

In the beginning the canal was used extensively by passenger boats as the quickest and most comfortable way to travel between Glasgow and Edinburgh. In 1848 the Canal Company stopped its passenger service, since by this time the Edinburgh-to-Glasgow

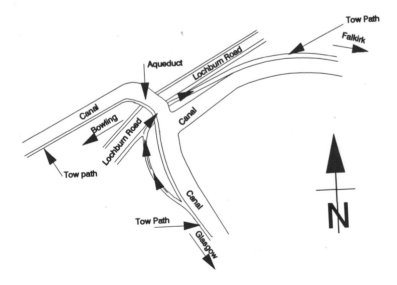

Railway had opened, and most people wanted to travel by train. Other companies ran passenger services until 1876. Pleasure steamers were introduced in 1893 and this service only ended at the beginning of the Second World War.

Until recently, the canal was bounded by factories manufacturing rubber products, oil by-products, a dye works, grain mills, and a distillery. In its heyday this part of the canal would have been bustling with barges and other traffic using Port Dundas and serving the factories. Sadly, much of this industry has now disappeared. This has been beneficial in one way, however, because the factories have stopped depositing harmful waste into the canal and it now supports varieties of flora and fauna unknown for the last 150 years.

The towpath is on the south bank of the canal and can be reached in many places along the first two miles of its length by Craighall Road, Possil Road, Garscube Road, Firhill Road, Ruchill Street or Lochburn Road.

Travelling west along the towpath, the first thing you will see is that the canal is set quite high, giving a good view over the city centre. On the left you will see Firhill Stadium, the home of one of Glasgow's famous football clubs, Partick Thistle, while on the right is Firhill Timber Basin, which was used to store logs until they were required by the sawmills.

Where the canal runs under Firhill Road, you will come upon the first of the two new bridges within Glasgow which have been reconstructed by the British Waterways Board (the other is at Ruchill Street). These bridges have been constructed in place of the culverts which were built when the canal was closed in 1963, which in their turn replaced the original bascule bridges. These works have been completed as part of the Glasgow Canal Project which was started in 1988, jointly funded by the British Waterways Board, Strathclyde Regional Council and the Manpower Services Commission. Its aim is to reopen 12 miles of the canal to shipping through the reconstruction of three bridges (thus increasing headroom) and replacing the lock gates at Maryhill. When the work is completed (much of it is already finished) pleasure boats will once again be able to sail all the way from Kirkintilloch to the heart of Glasgow, and from there west to Anniesland.

Even before reaching Ruchill, many varieties of water-fowl will be spotted on the canal, among them swans, ducks, moorhens and coots.

Carry on another quarter of a mile to Stockingfield, to where the Glasgow branch joins the main canal.

THE MAIN CANAL WEST

On the way west, on the main canal, after passing over Maryhill Road by way of the aqueduct, the first interesting feature reached is the Maryhill Lock Flight. This is the highest part of the canal, the summit level being some 156ft above sea-level. The locks were built by Robert Whitworth, the second chief engineer employed by the Forth and Clyde Canal Company to oversee the construction of the canal, which was finally finished by him in 1790.

As well as this flight of locks, Maryhill Docks was also constructed. This area is known locally as the Botany, for it was one of the points of embarkation for criminals deported to Botany Bay in Australia. Maryhill Docks was also a busy shipbuilding centre, where many of the Clyde puffers were built.

In the early part of the nineteenth century Maryhill was a sizeable industrial town. It is said that the original name for this area was Kelvin Dock, but the name Maryhill actually precedes this. In 1793 a feu was drawn up by Mary Hill, the proprietrix of Garbraid House, and her husband Robert Graham in favour of Robert Craig, that '32 Falls 11 Yards of land from the Glasgow boundary to Garscube Bridge be used to build a town and that this town be known henceforth as Maryhill'.

After passing the locks we very quickly come to the Kelvin Aqueduct, an important and imposing structure, best seen at the lower level which is conveniently on another walkway along the banks of the River Kelvin. The aqueduct carries the Forth and Clyde Canal 75ft above the river on a 400ft-long four-arched stone structure completed in 1790, which is still doing its job today without any visible signs of distress.

After crossing Cleveden Road the way continues, first past Cleveden Gas Works and then across a small aqueduct which takes the canal over a disused railway line. This line is to open again, to form part of the new light rail system which Strathclyde Regional Council will build as part of the city's public transport system for the twenty-first century. It will take trams from Anniesland to Maryhill.

Around this part of the canal is a pub called Lock 27 which is right on the towpath and is named after the lock nearby. On a summer's day it is pleasant to sit outside and enjoy life around the canal.

The canal passes under Bearsden Road to Temple, North Knightswood, and goes on to Garscadden where, alas, in 1963 it was filled in for a distance of about quarter of a mile. It reappears again once Great Western Road has been crossed. At the place where the canal disappears into the culverts, the Glasgow to Bearsden and Milngavie pathway, and the West Highland Way, which have been sharing the towpath since lock 27, leave it to go in a northerly direction, and will be described in a later chapter.

Two miles along the towpath is Clydebank. It was here that three great ships of the Cunard Line – the *Queen Mary*, *Queen Elizabeth* and *Queen Elizabeth II* – were built at the famous John Brown Shipyard in the centre of Clydebank. The town itself was built in the late nineteenth century around the shipyards, grew as they grew, and almost died when they closed in the 1970s. The town has made great efforts to survive, however, and has guaranteed its future by attracting new industry to the area.

Because of the large concentration of heavy industry, Clydebank suffered very badly during the Second World War. Between 13 and 14 March 1941, German planes dropped hundreds of tons of bombs on the town, killing 534 people and injuring 790 more, with 4,300 houses destroyed, and another 7,700 badly damaged; in all, only eight houses in the town were left standing intact. It was a wonder that, relatively speaking, so few people were killed or injured. Surprisingly, the Nazi bombers caused very little damage to the town's industry, which was their target.

The Glasgow-to-Killin cycleway joins the canal towpath at Clydebank, and follows along its banks until it finishes at Bowling.

The canal crosses Dumbarton Road at Dalmuir and continues close to the River Clyde. It passes under the Erskine Bridge which carries traffic high above the river at Old Kilpatrick. Old Kilpatrick means 'the church of St Patrick', who is said by some historians to have been born in this area. Others say he was born further east in New Kilpatrick beside the loch of St Germains, now in Bearsden. The lands around Old Kilpatrick once belonged to Paisley Abbey and were considered a holy place.

Between Old Kilpatrick and Bowling lies Chapelhill, the western extremity of the Antonine Wall. When the canal was being dug, navvies found many Roman artifacts which can be seen at the Hunterian Museum at Glasgow University.

The canal ends at Bowling where it joins the River Clyde. The entrance is linked to the Clyde and Bowling Harbour by two sea locks, and is still being used by boats as a winter berth.

There is an old customs house to the north of the basin at Bowling. A massive railway swing bridge can also be seen. It was built for the Lanarkshire and Dunbartonshire Railway and opened in 1896. Beyond the railway bridge is the best-preserved of the hand-operated bascule bridges once found all along the length of the canal.

THE MAIN CANAL EAST

At Stockingfield junction, in order to get on to the eastern towpath, the traveller must go down the ramp on to Lochburn Road, turn right under the canal bridge and, staying on the same side of the road, go up the ramp to the towpath on the other side of the canal.

After a mile or so, the canal passes under Balmore Road Bridge into the district of High Possil, passing near Possil Loch

Mort-safe and watch-house, Cadder Church

a large area of marsh. This is a Scottish Wildlife Trust Reserve, and has huge stocks of wild-fowl wintering and breeding there. Carrying on for almost two miles to Balmuildy Road, you will reach Bishopbriggs Sports Centre which, along with its café and bar, has a large swimming pool and a wide range of sports facilities.

A further mile takes the traveller to Cadder, which has a very interesting church and graveyard. At the beginning of the nineteenth century, doctors and surgeons were very keen to find out how the human body worked and to do this they had to have a large supply of bodies to dissect. To satisfy the growing demand certain enterprising and unscrupulous men supplied these bodies – either stealing corpses before burial, digging the bodies up after they were buried, or even in some cases resorting to murder. The most famous of these 'bodysnatchers' were Burke and Hare. Because of its proximity to the canal Cadder Church was an ideal spot for bodysnatching – the canal being a fast and convenient way to transport corpses to Edinburgh or Glasgow as the need arose. Indeed, this happened so often that the people of Cadder had a watch house built and had iron mort-safes constructed to protect their coffins from attack, and these can still be seen in the churchyard. In 1820 a ship docked at Liverpool was found to contain a cargo of bodies which were thought to have come from Dublin. The cargo was labelled 'Bitter Salts' and was bound for Edinburgh through the canal. Thomas Muir, the Scottish leader of the eighteenth-century campaign for parliamentary reform, was once an elder at Cadder Church. At this time he lived in Bishopbriggs at Huntershill House, now a museum devoted to his life and work.

Born in Glasgow in 1765, Muir studied divinity at Glasgow University and law at Edinburgh, being admitted to the Faculty of Advocates in 1787. He gained a reputation for having strong principles and soon built up a good legal practice. He often represented the poor, one of the very few of his profession who did. Many of his clients were strikers and others with grievances against the political system of the time. He mixed with people who were no lovers of the Union and who were greatly influenced by the French Revolution, believing that political reform was also urgently required in Scotland. Muir began to correspond with French revolutionaries and in 1792 set up the Edinburgh Friends of the People. At the organisation's first National Convention in December 1792, the authorities, who were nervous of any form of agitation, arrested Muir and others, charging them with sedition. On bail in London pending his trial, Muir heard that the French were about to execute King Louis and the French royal family. Fearing this could have a disastrous effect on the Revolution by causing a political split within France and deterring people from joining the reforming movements in Britain, he set off to France to state his case but arrived too late to prevent the executions. He was delayed in France and failed to appear on the day fixed for his trial. On his return he was immediately arrested and imprisoned in the Tolbooth in Edinburgh. Sentenced to 14 years' deportation, Muir and other leaders of the Scottish reform movement were sent out to Botany Bay in Australia in 1794.

He managed to escape on an American ship after 16 months in the penal colony. His idea was to get to Philadelphia where he intended to join George Washington whom, he felt, would welcome him as a brother revolutionary.

He never reached Philadelphia, ending up instead, through a series of mishaps, first in Mexico, then Spain, and finally France, where he received a hero's welcome. He settled in Paris and from there continued to support the radical movements from afar, liaising between the French Government and British and Irish political exiles. He became more and more radical in his ideals and sought the French Government's military support in establishing republics in Scotland, Ireland and England which, of course, never took place. Later Muir moved to Chantilly and there in 1799 he died at the age of 33.

A memorial was erected in his honour in Edinburgh by the Friends of Parliamentary Reform in England and Scotland and the inscription quotes words spoken by Muir at his trial: 'I have devoted myself to the cause of the People; it is a good cause; it shall finally triumph.'

The Forth and Clyde Canal at Glasgow Bridge

From Cadder the towpath continues to Glasgow Road Bridge. From 1831 until 1848 a fleet of horse-drawn boats called 'swifts' – because of their speed – sailed between Glasgow and Falkirk. In order to maintain their high speed (around ten miles per hour), the horses towing the boats had to be changed regularly. The fine Georgian building now converted into the Stables restaurant and bar was the place where horses were exchanged. This building was restored in 1981, around the same time as boats returned to the canal. A restaurant barge and some pleasure boats operate from here, but with Glasgow Bridge now finished (the third of the new bridges mentioned earlier), these boats can once again continue to Kirkintilloch, just over a mile further on.

From the twelfth century this area and all the way to Cumbernauld was in the hands of the Comyn family who had their castle at Kirkintilloch. The moat is still visible at Peel Park. William Comyn granted burgh status to the town in 1211, although it dates back much further than that. Its name was originally Caerpentulach – 'the fort on the ridge' – the 'fort' being part of the Antonine Wall.

Kirkintilloch remained a small agricultural and weaving community until the advent of the canal, and the town owes much of its development to this waterway. In 1773 while work had stopped on the canal further west, Kirkintilloch was operating as Scotland's first inland port through its access to the River Forth and the east. In 1860 the first shipbuilding and repair yard was opened and shipbuilding went on in Kirkintilloch until the Second World War.

Sadly, the canal is still culverted under Townhead in Kirkintilloch, but just beyond this point a new bridge has been constructed, part of the Kirkintilloch Relief Road Project, which has sufficient headroom to let boats through. Perhaps another bridge will be built at Townhead.

The canal goes on by way of Twechar, a small mining and quarrying village, and passes close to Barr Hill and Croy Hill, each of which has a Roman fort. This area possessed good stretches of the Antonine Wall which can be seen within a short distance from the canal. To reach them, cross the canal at the bridge in Twechar. Continue on the left side of the road for about 100m to where a track goes off to the right. Follow this track for a quarter of a mile up a long hill until a covered circular concrete reservoir is reached. At this point take the path to the left, through a gate, and continue on another 50m to Barr Hill Fort. It is a worthwhile detour as there is a great deal to see: the layouts of the fort and bath-house are clearly defined, with some of the stonework still in place. Carry on to the top of the next hill – marked by a concrete cairn – to the site of an Iron Age fort which predates the Roman one. From here the ditch in front of the wall is clearly visible. There is also a very good view of the canal and the surrounding countryside below.

Follow the path, continuing in the direction you have come, skirting a wood on the right, on down the hill, soon joining a larger path which in turn joins the A802 at Croy. Here turn left and very soon, at Auchinstarry, the canal is once again reached, and the way continues. The canal passes under the B802 Kilsyth to Cumbernauld road at Auchinstarry, and is spanned by a non-opening bascule bridge.

Some 300m away in the direction of Kilsyth is a disused quarry which has been turned into a leisure area by Kilsyth and Cumbernauld District Council. The floor of the quarry is under water, and this small lock has landscaped areas in the foreground with a 100ft-high whinstone face as a backdrop. It is very pleasant to see a disused industrial site – previously a blot on the landscape – turned into such an attractive and interesting place. The whinstone or dolerite which was quarried here was worked into kerbs and paving stones, which were taken on barges along the canal to pave the streets of Glasgow.

On another mile and a half to Craigmalloch where the canal crosses the road to Dullatur. This is where the main source of water enters the canal, the inlet being right beside the road and running in a lade from Banton Loch a mile to the north. Banton Loch, or Townhead Reservoir as it is also known, is in its present form man-made, and is a very picturesque loch with a pleasant walk around its banks. The locals use it extensively for fishing, but are always complaining that they never catch anything. The loch is reached from the canal by first turning north about half a mile to the A803 Kilsyth to Falkirk road. On reaching the A803, an unsignposted track can be seen opposite; take this track for a quarter of a mile, where the south-west side of the loch is reached. Continuing further north on this track leads to the Kilsyth Hills, where there are many fine walks into the Campsie Fells, through the Carron Valley Forest and Loch Carron. Even if you are not in the mood for a long climb, it is interesting to walk on for a mile or so, just to see the spectacular view over practically the whole of the Forth and Clyde Valley.

Kilsyth also lies to the north about half a mile away, and can be reached easily from either Craigmalloch or Auchinstarry. There are many explanations of the town's name. The most popular view is that *kil* means 'church' or 'chapel', and *sythe* is a reference to a mythical saint of that name. Others think that it changed its name in the sixteenth century from Monieburgh which meant 'hilly place of streams'. The true definition, however, is that there were two estates adjoining one another, the westerly Kelvesith (meaning 'Kelvin Sands') being changed over the years to the present Kilsyth. The estate to the east was indeed Moniebrugh. In 1620 Sir William Livingston, the owner of Kilsyth Castle since the beginning of the century, acquired the Moniebrugh estate as well, and the two were merged, with the whole area being known as Kilsyth.

The Battle of Kilsyth, which was part of the Civil War, was fought close to the town in 1645. Around the reservoir area are places named Slaughter Howe, Bullet Knowe and Drum Burn, testifying to the ferocity of the battle. The Marquis of Montrose with an army of Highlanders fighting on the side of Charles I had already seen many victories that year. These successes by Montrose were somewhat tempered by the defeat of King Charles's army at Naseby in June, and with no hope of victory left in England it made victory in Scotland all the more important. A Covenanter army of 10,000 troops had been mustered in Perth under General William Baillie, and had marched south to head off Montrose before he reached England. They met at Kilsyth on 15 August. In a final devastating surge with the battle becoming merely a slaughter of the Covenanter forces, Montrose's army of 5,000 men won the day. Baillie fled with a detachment of cavalry but was trapped in the nearby Dullater Bog. Some 125 years later, when the canal was being cut through the bog, a number of Baillie's unfortunate troopers were discovered exactly where they submerged, including one apparently still seated on his horse.

Dullater Bog was one of the most difficult obstacles encountered by John Smeaton while constructing the canal. The land was so wet and soft that nothing could be built on it without sinking, and it had to be completely drained. Unfortunately for the local inhabitants of Dullater, this disturbed millions of tiny toads from their natural environment in the bog and caused them to invade the houses and lands of the people living round about. So great was this problem that a complaint was sent to the canal authorities. Stone banks were then constructed which kept sinking into the ground. It was estimated that they sank to a depth of 50ft below ground-level in some places before they were consolidated and could form the actual canal bank.

Heading for Castlecary some five miles to the east of Kilsyth will take the traveller past the small village of Kelvinhead, the source of the River Kelvin in Dullatur Bog just to the south, and past another obstacle: the A80 Glasgow to Stirling road. Here is also found Wyndford Lock (Lock 20), the first for 16 miles since leaving Maryhill in Glasgow.

Castlecary takes its name from the castle built in 1473 by the Livingston family, and which is still standing today. It means 'the castle of the fort', and the castle itself was constructed from the stone of an old Roman fort.

A couple of miles further on is the Underwood Lockhouse, formerly the home of the lock-keeper, and now a very fine bar and restaurant offering a welcome break from the canal-side journey.

From here it is not long before an aqueduct is reached which takes the path beneath the canal to Seabegs Wood. The Antonine Wall* runs adjacent to the canal at this point and is very clearly defined. This is the site of a fortlet excavated in 1977 which is well worth a look.

The route passes High Bonnybridge, a small mining and foundry town, from where another Roman fort can be reached: Rough Castle is a 20-minute walk from the canal, and is clearly signposted. Access is along a farm road, then via a rough track to a carpark. Along the track is Bonnybridge House, and between this point and Rough Castle itself lies the best-preserved section of the Antonine Wall: the rampart and ditch, the remains of two signalling platforms, and even traces of the military way can be seen. Although one of the smallest forts along the length of the wall, Rough Castle offers the sightseer a very good picture of the fort and its defences. An unusual feature which can also be seen

---

*The Antonine Wall was built in AD 142 on the orders of the Roman Emperor Antoninus Pius. It stretched for about 85km (36 miles) and construction was carried out by the three legions stationed in the area at the time. The legionaries were aided by large numbers of slave labourers from the local communities in building the wall, which was mainly earth turfed over on a stone base. There was also a huge ditch in front of the wall, sometimes as much as 40ft wide and 12ft deep. Unfortunately little trace of the wall remains today, apart from the occasional fort.

is the pits dug in the north-west corner of the site. Each pit contained a sharpened stake concealed below ground-level, and was designed to prevent any attack on the vulnerable gateway through the wall. Finds from the fort can be seen in the Royal Museum of Scotland in Edinburgh.

Back to the canal as it crosses the B816 at High Bonnybridge, one should look out for a colourful mural on the exterior walls of the foundry by the bridge over the canal.

Three miles further on takes the towpath to Falkirk via Camelon. Falkirk (or Fawe Kirk, meaning 'speckled church') has been a burgh since 1600. The town had been in existence for many centuries before that date, however, and has had more than its fair share of events that have shaped Scotland's history. As well as being the site of a Roman fort, the town also gave its name to two famous battles, although the actual geographical locations of these could hardly be said to be in Falkirk itself.

The first battle was in 1298 when William Wallace's forces fought the biggest English army to be assembled thus far in Scotland – 25,000 infantry and almost 6,000 cavalry – under Edward I, the so-called 'Hammer of the Scots'. The Scottish forces were not united, however; most of the noblemen fighting at Wallace's side were from Noman families and had previously fought for the English king. Many of them were jealous of Wallace's position as Guardian of Scotland because he was a commoner. Wallace's forces sustained dreadful losses due in part to the desertion of his knights, and the graves of many of the fallen Scots can still be seen in the old churchyard in Falkirk.

After the battle was over many of the Scottish knights who had fled the scene went to Edward to plead for forgiveness. One of these was Bruce who, at Bannockburn a few years later, would once and for all teach Edward that he was not the 'Hammer of the Scots'.

The outcome of the second Battle of Falkirk, in January 1746, could not be more different. While the first was defeat for the Scots, the second saw them victors. Bonnie Prince Charlie's Jacobite forces defeated the Government troops led by General Hawley on a day of gale force winds and driving rain. Their victory was short-lived, however, as a mere three months later, on 16 April 1746, the Jacobites were resoundingly beaten at Culloden by an army commanded by the Duke of Cumberland who had been sent north to replace the disgraced Hawley. Bonnie Prince Charlie made good his escape and lived as a fugitive for a year, eventually being taken to safety in France, and the Jacobite cause was finally defeated.

Falkirk became famous for the Tryst, which was the national meeting place for the sale of farm animals and the gathering place for drovers and dealers from all parts, from the Western Isles and Ross-shire in the north to Yorkshire in the south. The fair, first held on Redding Moor just south of Falkirk, was then moved to Rough Castle and later, in 1785, was transferred to its final location in Stenhousemuir, where it remained till 1900. There were no auctioneers and cattle were sold only after a bargain was struck between the dealer and the drover and a 'dram' was drunk. The Tryst took place on the second Tuesday of August, September and October. Today it is limited to a single weekend, which it shares with the fair.

In the eighteenth and nineteenth centuries Falkirk was the centre of the iron industry in Scotland, due to the plentiful supply of iron ore being mined in the district, and many companies used the canal to transport their products. Today Falkirk is a fine town, mixing the modern with the traditional. Most of the industry in the area is confined to Grangemouth and other surrounding areas.

Nowadays the Forth and Clyde Canal ends its 35-mile journey in Falkirk, the last few miles to the River Forth being culverted. Before it finishes it descends through a picturesque series of locks, starting at Lock 16. Opposite these locks is the Union Inn, from where the Forth and Clyde Canal was linked to the Union Canal at Greenbank. If the traveller wishes to continue the journey east to Edinburgh along the banks of the Union Canal, then there are over 30 interesting miles to go.

Please note that if you are cycling along the length of the canal bank, British Waterways require a permit costing £3, except where the path is publicly owned.

CHAPTER 6

The Glasgow to Bearsden and Milngavie Cycleway
and Associated Walkway to the Kilpatrick Hills and West Highland Way

This route follows parts of different pathways and rights-of-way which conveniently join together to form a very important link in the north-west of Glasgow and beyond. It starts at two points within the city. The first is on the Clyde Walkway anywhere on the Broomielaw within the city centre, which then goes on to the Glasgow-Loch Lomond Cycleway. The second is from the Forth and Clyde Canal at Port Dundas just north of the city centre. Both the canal and the cycleway have been described in previous . chapters, so this description will begin from the points where this new route starts.

The route leaves the cycleway at Primrose Street, Scotstoun, for a distance of 150m, crosses Dumbarton Road and continues alongside a bowling green. Through the underpass below the Clydeside Expressway, the route continues in a roughly north-easterly direction past a football field and under a bridge which spans Danes Drive. From this point there is easy access to Victoria Park, another of Glasgow's many beautiful parks. Built partly on the site of an old quarry, it is renowned for its formal rock gardens and arboretum. Most famous of all is the Fossil Grove uncovered in 1887, a unique geological example of

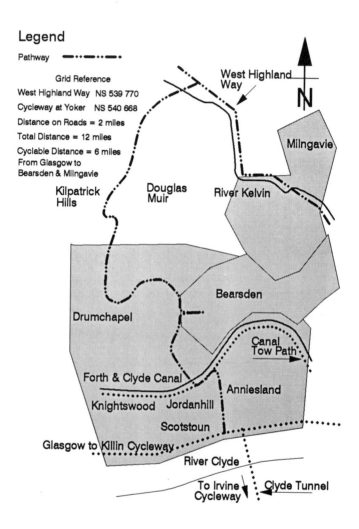

Legend

Pathway ━ ·· ━ ·· ━ ·

Grid Reference
West Highland Way NS 539 770
Cycleway at Yoker NS 540 668
Distance on Roads = 2 miles
Total Distance = 12 miles
Cyclable Distance = 6 miles
From Glasgow to
Bearsden & Milngavie

West Highland Way

N

Milngavie

Kilpatrick
Hills

Douglas
Muir

River Kelvin

Bearsden

Drumchapel

Canal
Tow Path

Forth & Clyde Canal

Anniesland

Knightswood

Jordanhill

Scotstoun

Glasgow to Killin Cycleway

River Clyde

To Irvine
Cycleway

Clyde Tunnel

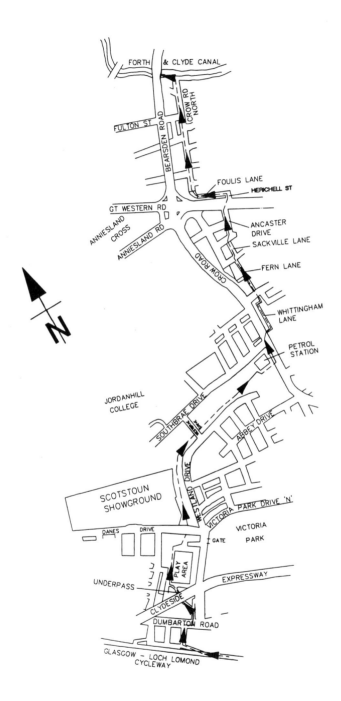

petrified tree stumps and roots which grew some 250 million years ago. The way continues past Scotstoun Show Ground and goes under another bridge at Westbrae Drive. Jordanhill College can be easily reached from here. Just past this point the track becomes less formal, although cycling is still possible with care. It is not much more than 500m to Crow Road. Turn left on to this very busy and dangerous road, cross Southbrae Drive and then Crow Road itself, and continue for a further 50m. Turn right into Whittingham Lane and follow Fern Lane and Sackville Lane to Ancaster Drive and thus to Anniesland Cross. Here cross Great Western Road into Herichell Street and turn left to Foulis Lane. This leads to Crow Road North and on to the towpath of the Forth and Clyde Canal, where the route merges with that from Port Dundas.

Carry on along the towpath for a further mile and a half to where the canal disappears into a culvert at Blairdardie Road. Double back on to Moraine Avenue past a small roundabout, through a pedestrian lane for 20m and under a railway bridge. If cycling, obey the sign to dismount along the path, turn right on to Essenside Avenue for 100m and then on to the path again to where it crosses Drumchapel Road. Strathclyde Regional Council and Glasgow City Council have plans to formalise this route, so some of these convoluted detours should be ironed out.

From now on the route becomes more straightforward. It has become a formal, signposted cycle/footpath, and it is fast leaving the city behind with only the boundary of Drumchapel, a huge housing estate built in the 1950s, to pass. In fact, we have Drumchapel to thank for the footpath itself, as it was built as part of the Kilpatricks Project for urban renewal in the area. This path orbits almost the whole of Drumchapel at the moment and there are plans for it to be completed at some point in the future.

Although Drumchapel is a fairly modern housing estate, the area has a very interesting history. In Roman times, the Antonine Wall was built only yards from Drumchapel's northern boundary. The name Drumchapel is derived from the two drums (or ridges) which bound the area: one is known as Drumry and the other as the Drum of the Chapel. The chapel is the Chapel of St Mary,

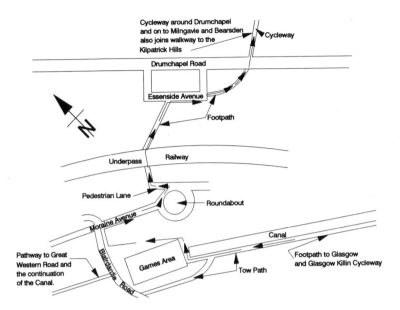

built in the fifteenth century in the ancient village of Drumry. Drumry at Kingsridge is said to be where an ancient Celtic-British chief made his permanent encampment. There is also evidence of druids in this area.

If you want to go to Bearsden, turn right at Colquhoun Park after about 500m from the start of the cycleway on Drumchapel Road. This leads into Bearsden. My route uses this path for about a mile through Garscadden Wood, to where the path splits in two. Take the right-hand path to Peel Glen Road. At this point cyclists have to leave the pathway. Those cycling to Milngavie should turn right on to Peel Glen Road, then left on to Duntocher Road for a distance of about 200m, and then right again on to the B8050 which continues past the roundabout on the Stockie Muir road and on to Milngavie.

If you are going to the Kilpatricks, turn right on to Peel Glen Road, then left on to Duntocher Road. Go past the B8050 and take Cochno Road, the next road to the right, a very quiet C-class road where the cyclist should not find much conflict with motor vehicles. Heavy traffic will, however, be encountered on Dun-

77

tocher Road and the B8050. I would suggest the cyclist use the pavement wherever possible, taking care to avoid pedestrians. Continue along Cochno Road for some two miles to where the road passes a water treatment plant. There, take the road to the right which will, within a mile, revert to a substantial pathway going to Greenside Reservoir and on into the Kilpatrick Hills.

As for those on foot, the path becomes less obvious after crossing Peel Glen Road. If you are in any doubt just follow the electricity pylons for a short distance and very soon the path will once again become apparent. All around are traces of the Antonine Wall.

The path is signposted as a right-of-way and swings to the east for about a quarter of a mile before turning north again until it comes out on to Duntocher Road by way of a stile. Cross Duntocher Road into Cochno Road and go on for about three-quarters of a mile to where the path is once again signposted as a right-of-way leading to Milngavie and Bearsden.

About 10m further on, on the other side of the road, is the entrance to a network of footpaths and pleasant walks in the countryside through the area around Faifley known as Auchna-craig Park.

After Cochno Road the right-of-way follows a northerly route, climbing high over Douglas Muir. When you reach the highest point, turn round to see the splendid view over the Clyde Valley which, on a fine day, can be quite spectacular. The path is easy to follow all the way to the Stockie Muir road. After crossing this road and entering Craigton Wood, the path splits in two. One fork heads south-east straight into Milngavie via Craigton Road, while the other fork goes east for a short distance past a farmhouse called Low Craigton, and then north again past a dam across Cauldstream Burn to a stone bridge. It then goes on to Craigallian Road, continuing for half a mile to where the West Highland Way crosses. Alternatively, one can walk another half a mile along this road to where the entrance to Mugdock Park at the Khyber carpark is reached. Continuing a little further still to where a stile can be seen on the left connects with the walkway to Strathblane and is described in the next chapter.

CHAPTER 7

The West Highland Way to Strathclyde Park Walkway

This walkway is the link from the West Highland Way to the Clyde Walkway at Strathclyde Park, skirting around the north and east of Glasgow.

The route starts at Carbeth. Leave the West Highland Way just 100m after it crosses the B821, by a footpath which forks to the left. The path, though wide and clearly defined, rises through thick forest for about half a mile to where it comes to a T-junction. At this point, turn right (turning left will take you to Mugdock, as described in Chapter 8) and follow the path for almost two miles to Strathblane, winding down through the upper part of the village via Old Mugdock Road and Dumbrock Road, to where the junction of the A81 (Glasgow-Aberfoyle road) and the A891 (Strathblane-Lennoxtown road) is reached. Turn along the right-hand side of the A891 for some 50m, to where the path recommences on the right. Walk down this path for 100m until it meets the disused Gartness to Kirkintilloch Railway which runs parallel to the road. This stretch, recently completed, goes from Strathblane to just beyond Moodiesburn, affording the traveller many comfortable miles.

After about two-and-a-half miles, the way crosses a farm road

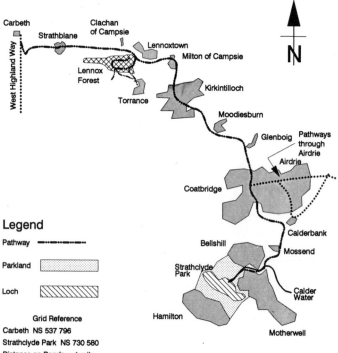

Carbeth

Clachan
of Campsie

Strathblane

Lennoxtown

Milton of Campsie

West Highland Way

Lennox
Forest

Torrance

Kirkintilloch

Moodiesburn

Glenboig

Pathways
through
Airdrie

Airdrie

Coatbridge

Calderbank

Bellshill

Mossend

Strathclyde
Park

Calder
Water

Hamilton

Motherwell

N

Legend

Pathway ━━•━•━•━•━•━•••━

Parkland

Loch

Grid Reference
Carbeth NS 537 796
Strathclyde Park NS 730 580
Distance on Roads = 1 mile
Total Distance = 26 miles
Cyclable Distance = 26 miles

which goes to Clachan of Campsie, the first of many access routes into the Campsie Hills. The ninth-century St Machan, who is said to be one of the earliest native-born evangelists, built the first place of worship in the area there. In 1175 a parish church was built on his grave, replaced after the Reformation by another church on the same site. Only a gable is left standing today. The graveyard has the Lennox family's mausoleum which dates back many centuries. Among other interesting people also buried there are John Bell, the Court Physician to the Russian King Peter the Great, and William Boick, Covenanter and martyr.

A little further on is Lennox Castle, the seat of the Lennox family until it was sold in 1927. Glasgow Corporation developed the building as a hospital for the mentally ill in 1937, and it is still used for this purpose today.

The way goes on via the village of Lennoxtown (previously known as Newton of Campsie); it was once noted for calico printing and hand-loom weaving, industries which nowadays have completely vanished. Lennoxtown is another place where the traveller can gain access to the Campsie Hills.

Just before reaching the village, the traveller will come to the second bridge over the path (the first being at Lennox Castle). Climb to the road above and turn right, following the road as it winds to the top of the hill to Lennox Forest. There are many walks through the woods here. At Muirhead Farm there is a signpost pointing out a right-of-way, down the valley to Torrance. Continue to follow the forestry road, keeping the radar station on the left. Here on a clear day it is possible to see over the entire city of Glasgow. Carry on till a single-bar gate across the road is reached; pass this, and carry straight on for another 200m. Take the road to the left and follow it as it winds downhill past a disused quarry on the right. This road is known as Mealy Brae. After about two miles or so this road comes out on to the A81 at the junction with the Mugdock road (which leads back to Mugdock Country Park, if so desired).

Two miles further on is Milton of Campsie, said to have been a great centre for whisky smuggling in the eighteenth century. From Milton it is barely a mile along a pleasant wooded path to

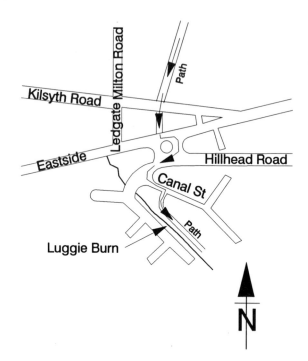

Kirkintilloch as the footpath joins the Kilsyth road.

The traveller should go by way of the path adjacent to Ledgate, across Eastside and into Canal Street. Here the footpath network recommences. Go on under the canal aqueduct, take the bridge over the Luggie Water, follow alongside it and double back over the burn again, by the next bridge. Go through an underpass under New Lairdsland Road, up a ramp into Industry Street and there the way is signposted as it enters Woodhead Park. After Woodhead Park the clearly defined footpath follows the line of the Monklands and Kirkintilloch Railway.

The four miles along the Bothlin Burn to Moodiesburn are picturesque. The outskirts of the town, where the path winds alongside a land-fill site, are not quite so pleasant, but this is only for a couple of hundred metres till the path crosses Gartferry Road.

The area here is known as Bridgend. This was a thriving mining village purpose-built in the early 1900s to serve Auchen-

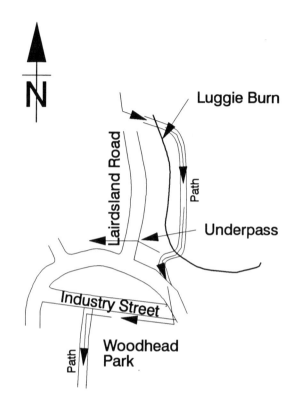

geich Colliery. After a serious fire in 1957 when 47 miners lost their lives and the colliery had to be flooded to extinguish the fire, it was never worked again. The community began to move away from Bridgend and by 1964 it was deserted, being demolished in 1967.

Once past Bridgend, the path once again joins the Bothlin Burn as it bisects the area between Moodiesburn and Cryston; it then goes on under the A80, continuing to follow the route of the dismantled railway.

The path officially ends about half a mile further on where it is cut by the Marnock to Moodiesburn road. The dismantled railway continues on the other side of the road, though, and the walker can follow it. After about quarter of a mile the railway is once again cut, this time by the M73, but there is not much of a

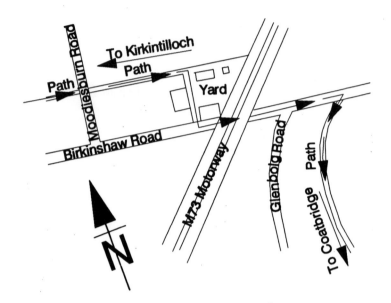

detour to get to the other side. Go by way of a factory yard which leads on to another part of the Marnock to Moodiesburn road, which in turns passes underneath the M73. Follow this road for about 100m to a T-junction. Pass this and continue on for another 100m to where the path starts again on the east side of the road. Follow this as it passes Marnock and Glenboig Loch, before crossing Glenboig Road and continuing on the other side of the road.

A mile further on the path enters Coatbridge, where it joins Gartgill Road. At this point the route continues for a mile or so by way of minor roads which rarely have much traffic, so the walker should experience little danger. The route is fairly straightforward, though care should be taken not to get lost. As the way joins Gartgill Road, continue straight on in the same direction as you have been travelling (not over the level crossing on the left) and carry on down this road over a railway bridge. About 100m beyond this bridge there is a fork in the road. Take the left fork at this point, although it appears to be almost the

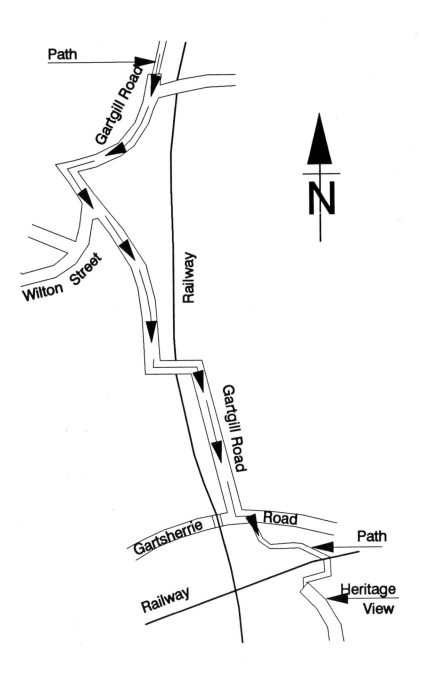

Path

Gartgill Road

Wilton Street

Railway

N

Gartgill Road

Gartsherrie   Road

Path

Railway

Heritage View

entrance to a yard. Follow the road for a mile to where it joins Gartsherrie Road. On the other side of Gartsherrie Road is the start of a formal walkway which should be followed. After a very short distance this path goes under a low railway bridge. At this point the walkway turns right and climbs a short but steep slope. Turn left at the top and, in a few metres, the walkway joins Heritage View leading on to Heritage Way.

At the end of Heritage Way is the entrance to one of Coatbridge's many attractions, Summerlee Industrial Museum, a very fine example of its kind. Located on the site of the former Summerlee Iron Works (which closed in 1932), it contains many exhibits on the area's industrial and sociological heritage, including the Monkland Canal, industrial archaeology, machinery, coalmining, locomotives, a row of nineteenth-century workers' cottages and, of course, several working tram cars. The museum is being extended all the time and is well worth a visit.

A very fine network of footpaths is contained within the town of Coatbridge. The entrance to these footpaths is on the other side of West Canal Street at the junction with Heritage Way. Access to the town's other leisure and recreation facilities can be gained from here. Just turn right following the path and within a very short distance the entrance to the Time Capsule can be seen on the left, on the other side of Bank Street. This leisure centre has been described as 'half ice, half water and a whole lot of fun' and I would agree with this. Continue in this direction and within a quarter of a mile the only part of the Monkland Canal still in existence within the centre of Coatbridge is reached. This part of the canal is very picturesque and its low path leads directly into Drumpellier Country Park.

The lands around Drumpellier were granted to the Cistercian monks of Newbattle Abbey in 1161 by Malcolm IV. The area was referred to as 'Munklands' in the Steward's Charter of 1323, which gave the monks the right of passage through the barony of Bathgate to their lands in the west. The monks farmed and dug for coal on this land until 1560 when, due to the Reformation, they were forced to sell it to the Duke of Hamilton.

The Monkland Canal, Coatbridge

The estate was sold several times until it was donated in 1919 to the town of Coatbridge for public recreation.

Back to the route: when the walkway off Gartsherrie Road is reached, turn left and go under a low railway bridge. Once on the other side, carry straight on up a ramp to a shopping centre carpark. Keep to the southern boundary where, at the end of this carpark, the formal walkway recommences. From anywhere in this area the town centre of Coatbridge is easily reached.

The name Coatbridge (given as 'Cottbrig' on General Roy's map of 1750) is said to come from a family called the Colts who owned land in the area. The 'bridge' was over the Luggie Burn. The town grew throughout the nineteenth century with the increase in coalmining in the area, and became a burgh in the 1880s, but by the early part of the twentieth century the steel industry was taking over as the area's biggest employer.

The route continues through a pleasant landscaped area for almost a mile. This area was the former Monkland Canal which was filled in during the 1960s.

There is an extensive network of paths and walkways in Coatbridge because of the large number of disused railway lines

87

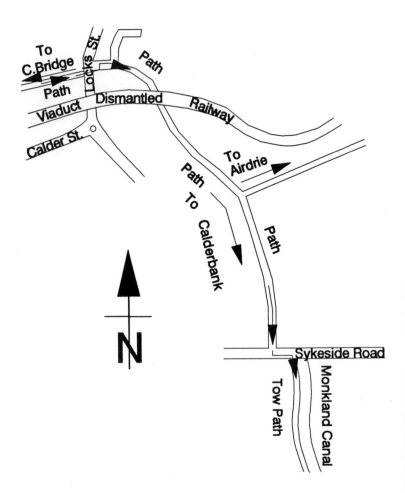

in the area. At one time every factory would have had its own railway siding to bring in raw materials and take away finished products. Until the 1960s this whole area was a vast concentration of heavy industry. At night the sky would have been lit up by blast furnaces, and the noise of steam-hammers would have been heard everywhere. It is hard to come to terms with the number of factories which have had to close in this area.

After passing Locks Road the pathway continues under a large viaduct. Less than 200m further on the path splits in two.

Keep to the right and continue to Sykeside Road. On the other side of this road the path joins the towpath of the Monkland Canal which at this point has reappeared above ground. The towpath follows the canal to Calderbank, a distance of approximately two miles.

The left fork in the path goes off in the direction of Airdrie, joining Cairnhill Road after half a mile. Follow in the direction of Airdrie town centre for no more than 200m to where, just after Cairnhill Avenue, a further series of paths begin. One of these goes towards the town centre, finishing at Gartlee Road. The others form links to all the housing estates in the area. Another path continues for quite some distance. It runs parallel to Ayr Drive until it reaches Calderbank Road. Cross this and the path continues, running parallel to this road until it has to cross it once again just to the north of Calderbank. On the other side of Calderbank Road the path recommences running east–west all the way to Chapelhall. Halfway along this stretch it crosses a path running north–south. On the north side this path ends at Monk Road, Airdrie, and on the south it terminates at Calderbank Road. The path to Chapelhall joins another path which runs parallel to the North Calder Water and goes almost all the way from the end of the Monkland Canal in Calderbank to the disused railway line which forms the Airdrie to Bathgate Cycleway.

On the east side of Airdrie at Drumgelloch Railway Station is the beginning of the Airdrie to Bathgate Cycleway. Presently under construction on the now disused section of the Glasgow to Bathgate railway, it is scheduled to be finished by 1994. Within this stretch an area between Blackridge and Caldercruix is now complete. This is the first stage of a cycleway which will be constructed all the way between Glasgow and Edinburgh to link the already completed cycleways in both the east and west of Scotland.

Back to the main route along the canal towpath to Calderbank. The canal finishes at the North Calder Water, where there is a timber bridge across the river. Cross this and climb a set of steps on the left. Turn hard right at the top and take a small

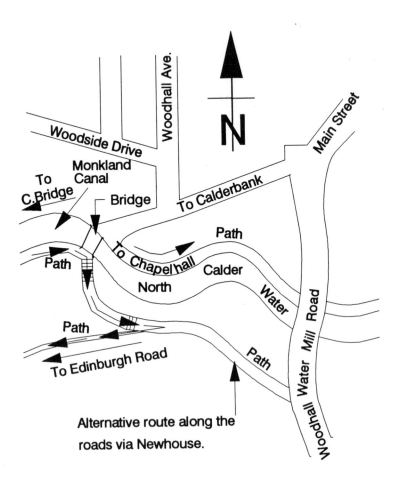

and sometimes very overgrown path for about half a mile. Here
the traveller will have to climb a gate beyond which there is a
short, steep slope to where the path connects with an unmade
estate road. When this road is reached, turn to the right and
follow it round until it joins another estate road. Turn to the left
at this point and carry on about half a mile to a T-junction. Turn
left and within 50m or so the Edinburgh road is reached. The
Edinburgh road (A8) is the only serious impediment that is met
in the entire 26-mile journey; as long as great care is taken when

crossing this dangerous road, it is not serious enough to stop the traveller reaching his or her destination. At the other side, the path is clearly defined and easy to follow until it reaches the A775 at Mossend.

For the next mile and three-quarters the way once again is on the road. Turn right and follow the A775 in the direction of Bellshill until a roundabout is reached. Turn left along the B7029, following the sign for New Stevenson and Carfin. In less than 200m another roundabout is reached. There are no signposts at this roundabout, so the traveller must take the second exit from the left. Keep to the left of this road and within about half a mile there is a gate which is the entrance to the walkway along the side of the South Calder Water. Within a very short distance this walkway goes under the A721 and out on to an access road. On the other side of this road are some steps back down to the river-bank. This is now the outermost extremity of Strathclyde Park.

Once in Strathclyde Park, the way is not difficult. Simply follow the path as it winds its way through the beautiful South Calder Valley.

Of particular interest are the sandstone cliffs which have been formed in the area known locally as Wallace's Cave. Nearby the path passes under the very high railway viaduct which carries electric trains from Motherwell to Glasgow. Another 500m further on, the path comes to a clearing. Here it starts to climb up through the gorge, temporarily leaving the riverside and passing Bellshill Golf Course on the right, past an area known as Orbiston Park and down to Spine Road.

On reaching the road, the Roman bridge over the Calder and a Roman bath-house are close by. There is also the remains of a fort, but there is not much of it to see and it is difficult to find. The Roman garrison was exactly one day's march to the south of the Antonine Wall, and although it was a fortification in its own right, it would also have served as a staging post for legionaries commencing or finishing a tour of guard duty at the wall.

Strathclyde Park is a junction where several walkways and cycleways converge and these are the subject of other chapters. At a local level the park allows direct access to the towns of

Roman bathhouse, Strathclyde Park

Motherwell, Hamilton and Bothwell. The park itself was opened in 1978 and lies in the valleys of the Clyde and the South Calder. It covers an area of some 1,650 acres and is without doubt one of Scotland's finest centres for outdoor activities. It has facilities for rowing, windsurfing, canoeing, dinghy sailing and water-skiing, football, rugby, hockey, cricket, golf, putting, tennis, bowling, jogging, orienteering, cross-country running, fishing and riding.

The area provides habitats for many species of birds both local and migrant, including some very rare varieties, and many miles of beautiful countryside in which to walk.

The walkway covered by this chapter is 26 miles long, going through several towns and both rural and industrial landscapes. In the miles between Moodiesburn and Motherwell, the traveller will have passed through the former industrial heartlands of Lanarkshire – from coal production in the north to steel production in the central area and the south.

Cardowan Colliery near Stepps, which was the last pit left in the area, closed in 1983. This has been followed by the closure of the many steelworks, culminating in the closure of Ravenscraig in June 1992. Only Dalzell Plate Works is left, its future hanging precariously in the balance. If it too closes, all the heavy industry for which this area has been renowned worldwide, will sadly have gone.

I managed to cycle this entire route and – with the exception of the path from the North Calder to the Edinburgh road, and once again at the start of Strathclyde Park where I had to dismount and walk – I experienced no great difficulty in doing so.

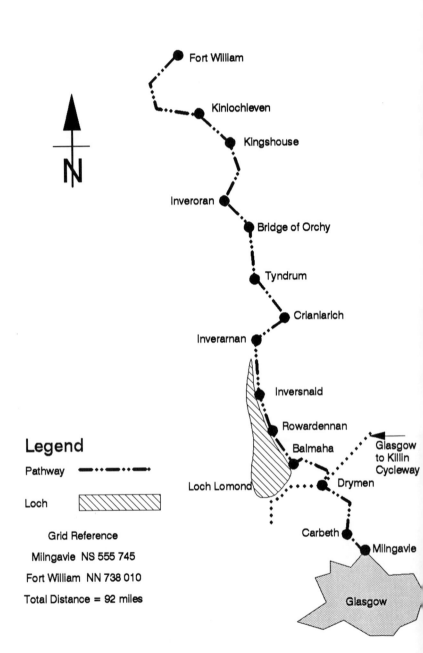

Fort William

Kinlochleven

Kingshouse

Inveroran

Bridge of Orchy

Tyndrum

Crianlarich

Inverarnan

Inversnaid

Rowardennan

Balmaha

Glasgow to Killin Cycleway

Drymen

Loch Lomond

Carbeth

Milngavie

Glasgow

N

Legend

Pathway

Loch

Grid Reference

Milngavie NS 555 745

Fort William NN 738 010

Total Distance = 92 miles

CHAPTER 8

The West Highland Way
and Associated Areas such as Mugdock

The West Highland Way was the first long-distance footpath to be opened in Scotland. Its official route is from Milngavie to Fort William, a distance of 92 miles. There has been much written over the years about this very fine footpath, not least the Countryside Commission for Scotland's official guide, a very helpful and concise book. For this reason I am not going to say much about it other than to explain how it forms part of the Glasgow network of footpaths, linking many in the area. It joins together the Kelvin Walkway and the Strathblane to Kirkintil- loch Walkway, for example.

One can simply use it from Milngavie to Carbeth and return at Carbeth Loch by climbing to the top path overlooking Craigallian Loch, which has been passed earlier on the West Highland Way. Take care not to enter the Craigallian Estate, but go on to Craigallian Road instead.

Join Mugdock Country Park at the Khyber carpark, from where a spectacular view over Glasgow can be had. Mugdock Country Park was opened in 1982 and was one of the first country parks in central Scotland. It contains many interesting features, such as Mugdock Castle which dates back to the

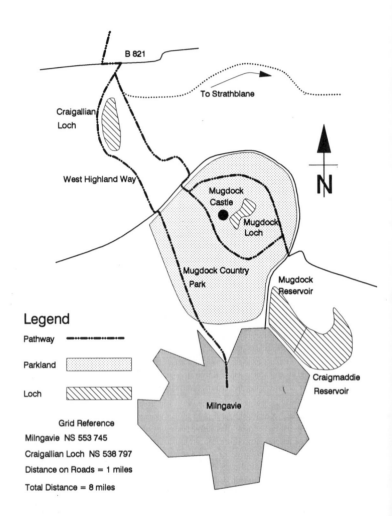

thirteenth century and belonged to the famous Graham family who feature so prominently in Scottish history. In 1644 the castle was extensively damaged by Covenanter forces sent by the Duke of Argyll after James Graham, the fifth Earl of Montrose, was declared a traitor. In 1649 Graham was tried in Edinburgh, and executed by being hanged and quartered. By this time, the castle had been awarded to Argyll, who held on to it until he was executed by Charles II in 1660, whereupon it then reverted back to the Grahams.

Other places of interest include Moothill, possibly the site of an ancient crannog and a medieval hill of judgment; Gallowhill, which until 1718 was the local place of execution; and Craigend Castle and Zoo, the castle being designed by James Smith of Jordanhill in 1818 for the Smith family, lairds of Craigend. The last laird died in 1851 and the estate was passed to Sir Andrew Buchanan, ambassador to the Viennese Court. In this century it was occupied by Sir Harold Yarrow, the Clyde shipbuilder, and George Outram, one of the former owners of the Glasgow *Herald* newspaper.

Mugdock Country Park is only eight miles from the centre of Glasgow and is well worth a visit.

From the Khyber Pass there are many ways to return to Milngavie. The shortest is to South Lodge past Mugdock Castle and then by Mugdock Road on to the walkway round the reservoirs of Mugdock and Craigmaddie (known to Glaswegians as 'the Waterworks') back on to Mugdock Road, and the last half-mile into Milngavie.

This is a distance of some eight miles, which I often use as a Sunday morning run. It is particularly interesting in winter when many species of wild animals come in close to Milngavie foraging for food. Within a mile of the town I have seen foxes, deer, herons and many birds of prey. On a sunny day the scenery around Craigallian Loch is most pleasing.

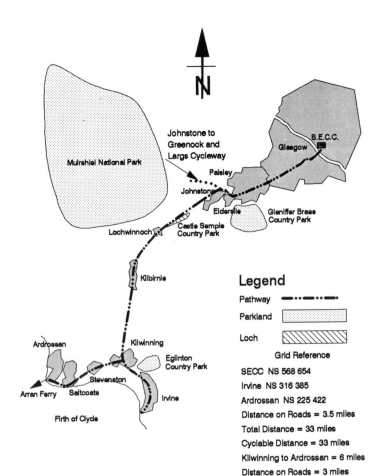

Johnstone to
Greenock and
Largs Cycleway

Muirshiel National Park

Paisley

Johnstone

Elderslie

Gleniffer Braes
Country Park

S.E.C.C.

Glasgow

Castle Semple
Country Park

Lochwinnoch

Kilbirnie

Kilwinning

Ardrossan

Eglinton
Country Park

Stevenston

Arran Ferry

Saltcoats

Irvine

Firth of Clyde

Legend

Pathway

Parkland

Loch

Grid Reference

SECC NS 568 654

Irvine NS 316 385

Ardrossan NS 225 422

Distance on Roads = 3.5 miles

Total Distance = 33 miles

Cyclable Distance = 33 miles

Kilwinning to Ardrossan = 6 miles

Distance on Roads = 3 miles

CHAPTER 9

The Glasgow to Irvine and Ardrossan Cycleway

This chapter deals with a route wholly on the south side of the River Clyde. After crossing the river there are no convenient parks, riverside footpaths or disused railway lines to connect the bridge with the adjoining cycleway further away on the south side. As a result, the cycleway has to take to the city streets, albeit for a short distance, until it reaches Bellahouston Park. It reverts back to public roads after this for short stretches along its route till it reaches Paisley. For the nine-mile stretch between Bell's Bridge and Paisley, I would suggest the cyclist mark out the route on a map before commencing.

The route crosses the river at Bell's Bridge, a fully operational swing bridge allowing shipping access upriver as far as the weir a half-mile beyond. These days this is normally confined to the Paddle Steamer *Waverley* and the occasional high-masted yacht.

After crossing the bridge the cycle track is well signposted through Govan and Kinning Park, and goes by way of Govan Road, Lorne Street, across Paisley Road, Clifford Street, and over Beach Avenue footbridge across the M8 motorway; it then turns right into Urrdale Road, across Dumbreck Road at the pedestrian crossing and enters Bellahouston Park.

Bellahouston Park is yet another of the city's 70 public parks. In 1938 the Empire Exhibition was held here, the centrepiece of which was a 300ft-high tower built on top of Bellahouston Hill, itself some 170ft above sea-level. It also had the biggest amusement park in Europe. Some 13,500,000 people visited the exhibition even though it rained almost every day. Another part of this exhibition was the Palace of Art, which still stands today.

Take the perimeter road around two sides of the park, passing the Palace of Art, and leave the park at the Mosspark Boulevard gate. Cross Mosspark Boulevard by the pedestrian crossing and turn left into the tree-lined Bellahouston Road. Cross Corkerhill Road at the traffic lights, continue down Kinnel Avenue and then left into Mosspark Drive. Follow close to the railway by way of Dundee Avenue to Berwick Drive and left into Cardonald Road, where Ross Hall Park is reached. Continue along the banks of the White Cart river to the junction at Crookston Road. Keep on the same side of the road, cross the bridge over the Cart and go under Crookston Road via the pedestrian tunnel, joining the river walkway once again on the south bank of the Cart.

At this point it is worth making a small detour: continue along Crookston Road for a few hundred metres to where Crookston Castle can be found. This fifteenth-century stone fortress, which was the residence of Sir John Stewart of Darnley (whose descendent Henry Stewart, Lord Darnley, married Mary Queen of Scots in 1565), stands on top of a defensive mound constructed in the twelfth century by Sir Robert Croc. Croc, a feudal tenant of the Royal House of Stewart, built a settlement next to his defensive mound, and it is from this – Croc's town – that Crookston derived its name.

Back on the south bank of the Cart, the route follows the river until it skirts around the grounds of Hawkhead Hospital, after which it comes out at Hawkhead Road. Note that about 300m on from Crookston Road, the way takes a right turn through a gate which could easily be missed. After crossing this road the route continues along the short Jenny's Well Road, at the end of which the path continues again until it joins Whinhill Road. Go straight on here to the junction of Cartha Crescent, turn right and follow this round in a half-circle, noting that at one point it changes its name to Cathcart Crescent. The path starts again, passing the imposing twelfth-century Blackhall Manor. A ruin until recently, it has been restored and is now a private dwelling house.

Within a very short distance the path joins and crosses Barrhead Road and goes by way of Ardgowan Street. Take the first road on the left (Hunterhill Road) and follow this to the end, where there is a small informal path leading to a grassy common. Once across the common there is a path which leads on to Causeyside Street. Here turn right down the hill and cross Causeyside Street by the pedestrian crossing. Turn right again, then quickly left into Stow Place. On the left is a pub which has been converted from the former Paisley Canal Street Station. Go through an opening into the beer garden at the rear of the pub where there is a path to the new station under Causeyside Street and the cycleway which follows the line of this now disused railway in the opposite direction.

Back on Causeyside Street, if the traveller wishes to get to Gleniffer Braes Country Park, turn left up Causeyside Street, Neilston Road, Stony Brae and Caplethill Road where there is an entrance to the park which extends for over a thousand acres. From this point on the cycleway becomes much easier to follow.

The traveller is now very close to the centre of Paisley. A settlement must have been here from prehistoric times, since its location close to the banks of two rivers would have been an important trading place. Christian Paisley was founded in 560 AD by an Irish missionary monk called Mirin, who set about building a small church on the east bank of the Cart. He stayed there till his death and was buried close to his church. He was said to have performed many miracles and, as St Mirren, became the patron saint of Paisley (hence the name of the local football team). His tomb became a place of pilgrimage and was considered important by the church of the day.

There is some debate about the origins of the town's name. Some think it was formed by joining two Brythonic Welsh words, *pasgell* ('pasture') and *lledh* ('plain' or 'field'), to give *Paslledh*. Others believe it is a corruption of the Latin *basilica*, meaning 'church', which would attest to Paisley's importance as a place of pilgrimage.

Until David I became King of Scots in the twelfth century, Scottish society was predominantly tribal. David had seen how the Anglo–Norman court of King Henry I operated, and he wanted the feudal system implemented in Scotland too. When he moved north to take up the Scottish crown, he brought with him many followers, among them the sons of Norman lords. David granted lands to these men, thus establishing feudalism in his kingdom. He also reduced the influence of the Celtic Church by promoting the Church of Rome with its structured hierarchy of bishops and abbeys.

One of Paisley's most notable features is its abbey which Walter Fitzalan founded in 1163 with 13 monks he had brought from a Cistercian order in Shropshire. It was damaged by fire, first by Edward I whose army set it alight in 1307, and then again in 1498. This second fire weakened the structure and led to the collapse of the central tower in 1540. Undaunted, the monks had it rebuilt. The monastery was closed in 1560 during the Reformation, when Paisley Abbey became a Protestant church.

King James IV granted a charter making Paisley a burgh of barony in 1488; it had previously been part of its much smaller neighbour, the Royal Burgh of Renfrew. From the eighteenth century, Paisley became famous for two industries – weaving and thread – which grew rapidly and brought more and more people into the area, enlarging the town substantially. Even now when, alas, most of the factories producing these fine products have closed, everyone knows about the famous Paisley Pattern. It imitates a Kashmiri pine pattern, which had a religious significance, and eighteenth-century travellers had introduced these patterns to the area when they brought back shawls from their travels in India.

I would recommend anyone wishing to explore this part of

the country to get a copy of the *Glasgow to Irvine Pedestrian and Cycle Route* brochures which are available from all tourist offices and regional and district council offices. They are very well produced and have detailed maps, so I don't intend to reiterate any of the information they contain. There are a few areas at various stages along the route where, mainly because of the theft of the direction signs, there could be some confusion as to the correct route. I will endeavour to shed some light on these problem areas as I come to them. As to the rest of the route, though, I shall confine my comments to places of interest along its length.

The next place to be passed after Paisley is Elderslie where, for a very short distance, the cycleway reverts to the streets (see map in brochure). Elderslie (previously known as Ellersly) was once an isolated village, but now forms part of the Paisley–Johnstone conurbation. It is, however, an historic place, with evidence of a settlement here going back to the Bronze Age, about 2,300 years ago. The best-known family to have lived in the area was the Wallaces of Ellersly. Their castle would have been situated where the Wallace Monument stands today. The first member of the Wallace family to settle in Scotland was Richard de Wals, a Norman knight who came north with David I in 1124 and settled in Ayrshire. It was his son, Sir Malcolm Wallace, who built the castle at Elderslie. He married Margaret Craufurd, the daughter of the Sheriff of Ayr, and their son William was born there in 1270. The death of King Alexander III in 1286 and the subsequent death of his only heir, the infant Margaret, on her return from Norway to take the crown, left the Scottish throne open to many contenders. The strongest of these were John de Bailleul (Balliol) and Robert de Brus (Bruce). King Edward I of England was asked by the Bishop of St Andrews to come to Scotland to keep the peace and to judge who was the strongest contender for the throne. He thought that Balliol would be more likely to acquiesce to his decisions on Scotland's future, so at Berwick Castle he declared Balliol king. Shortly after, Edward demanded that he was to become the feudal superior of Scotland and that Balliol should swear allegiance to him. Balliol refused, so Edward invaded Scotland and at Berwick in 1296, some 2,000 Scottish nobles and landowners were forced to pay homage to him and to sign a document recognising him as king.

Sir Malcolm Wallace refused to sign this document and the family were forced to flee. Young William and his mother went east, while his father and brother went north. Although still very young, Wallace had a deep loathing for the English invaders and, after his exploits at Lanark (see Chapter 1), he built up a strong army which annihilated a much larger English army at the Battle of Stirling Bridge in September 1297. In July 1298 he was badly defeated at Falkirk by Edward himself (see Chapter 5). For seven years he avoided capture, but in 1305 he was caught by the English and taken to London where, at a mock trial, he was sentenced to death, then barbarously executed by being hung, drawn and quartered, his head then nailed to London Bridge.

On the way from Paisley to Elderslie, various street names referring to a canal will be passed. The canal in question is the former Glasgow–Ardrossan Canal which was conceived by the Earl of Eglinton as a means by which goods could be transported speedily between Glasgow and the docks at Ardrossan. Designed by Thomas Telford, the Glasgow end of the canal was at Port Eglinton (now the approximate area of Eglinton Toll). It was only completed as far as Johnstone due to a lack of funds, and in 1810 it was opened to traffic. It was highly successful – at its peak, eight boats a day travelled in both directions, completing the journey in only one and a half hours. With the advent of the railways, however, the canal experienced a drop in popularity and in 1882 it was closed and later drained to make way for the Paisley to Kilmacolm railway – which in turn has now become the cycleway.

Where Main Road joins Canal Street the cycleway once again continues along the old railway towards Johnstone. In just over half a mile the way comes to the Johnstone Bypass where a footbridge now spans the new road. This is the junction of two cycle tracks; the one crossing the footbridge is to Kilmacolm and the other which continues along the east side of the bypass goes by Johnstone to Irvine. The Kilmacolm Cycleway is described in the next chapter.

Johnstone has been marked on maps for many hundreds of years. The Old Brig at Johnstone was the only place to cross the Black Cart river all the way to the River Clyde some miles to the north, so Johnstone would have been on the road through Renfrewshire from Paisley to Ardrossan. It was designed and built as a town in 1782 to house the families of the miners and quarriers who worked for George Houstoun Esquire, Laird of Johnstone. There was also a tradition of linen thread spinning, so the town grew rapidly during the Industrial Revolution. None of these industries exists today but Johnstone has seen a degree of regeneration with some new modern industrial estates being set up in and around the area.

Joined to Johnstone to the south-west is Kilbarchan. This was an eighteenth-century weaving village, and its two-storey houses were both home and weaving shop. One of these cottages has now been taken over by the National Trust for Scotland and completely restored to how it would have looked two centuries ago, its loom still in working order. Weaving demonstrations are given.

For the next four miles the route is through pleasant wooded countryside until it reaches Lochwinnoch; the latter two miles are along the banks of Castle Semple Loch. Lochwinnoch is where the traveller gains access to Scotland's first national park, a 14-mile area of countryside open to the public all the way from Lochwinnoch to Cloch Point on the Clyde coast, with nature trails, bird sanctuaries and a wilderness of moorland, rivers, lochs and woodland. As most of this land is privately owned, be vigilant, keep to the prescribed paths, keep control of your dog and don't start fires. Castle Semple Water Park is also part of the national park area and offers facilities for all sorts of watersports. The Royal Society for the Protection of Birds centre nearby has an observation tower, nature trails and birdwatching hides. These facilities are all well signposted from Lochwinnoch, which is itself an attractive rural village. It is worth noting, though, that the entrance to Muirshiel Park is some four miles from Lochwinnoch, leaving by way of the B786 Bridge of Weir road and then on to the unclassified road to Muirshiel.

For a short distance the cycleway leaves the line of the railway to circumvent Lochwinnoch. It soon joins it again on the other side of the village where there starts a four-mile uninterrupted stretch passing Barr Loch and Kilbirnie Loch. It then passes within a mile of the village of Kilbirnie, where the Stables Museum (only open by arrangement) and the Auld Kirk can be found. This church was completed in 1275 and is the oldest church in the area; it is also one of the oldest churches in Scotland still being used for worship.

From here the route reverts from pathway to minor road and careful note of the map must be taken for, unfortunately, there is a tendency for the signposts to be stolen. If there are signs missing, please inform the Regional Council Roads Department, who will replace them quickly. The next seven miles are on minor roads, and after crossing the A737 Dalry to Beith road, the route comes to a crossroads. Carry straight on here, for this is one place that seems to have its signs stolen with great regularity. I should also point out that there are fairly hilly sections on this part of the route.

At the end of this stretch is Kilwinning (meaning 'Church of Ninian' – St Ninian built a church here in the sixth century). Under the rule of David I, Kilwinning Abbey was built by Hugh de Morville in 1140 on the site of St Ninian's Church. It did not survive the Reformation, however, being partially destroyed in 1560 by the Earls of Arran, Argyll and Glencairn who, calling themselves the 'Lords of the Faithful Congregation' (self-styled defenders of the Protestant faith), set about reclaiming church lands 'usually for themselves'. Almost two miles outside Kilwinning, just off the A737 going in the direction of Dalry, is Dalgarven Mill, a water-mill built in 1620. Now fully restored as a working museum, the mill is once again grinding corn. The mill buildings also contain a museum of country life, a costume collection with over six hundred outfits dating from 1780, and a very fine bakery and coffee room. The mill can be reached directly from the cycleway without having to backtrack from

Dalgarven Mill

Kilwinning as follows: after crossing the A760 and following the minor road for just short of three miles, the road goes under a railway bridge. The cycleway is straight on, but if the little road off to the right is taken instead, this comes out directly at Dalgarven Mill, and there is therefore no need to use the busy A737. It is also another way to get to Kilwinning.

In Kilwinning itself the cycleway splits, one way going to Irvine and the other to Ardrossan. Although the cycleway here is generally well signposted, a handy tip is that when the traveller reaches the junction at Howgate, it is left for Irvine and right for Ardrossan.

After leaving Kilwinning behind and on route for Irvine, the traveller comes to Eglinton Country Park, a thousand acres of varying countryside opened in 1986. This land was the former Eglinton Country Estate and the seat of the Montgomeries, Earls of Eglinton. The Country Park has in essence kept the character of this estate and also tried to re-establish areas of hedgerows and woodland which had been removed in the nineteenth and twentieth centuries to make room for more farming land.

Irvine is a new town, developed from the 1946 Clyde Valley Plan which called for the establishment of new towns to relieve overcrowding in the existing communities in the Clyde Valley. It is not a completely 'new town', however, since traces have been found there of Stone Age hunters who visited the then arctic terrain foraging for food. As with all of West Central Scotland, the area was not colonised until much later, during the Bronze and Iron Ages. The name Irvine comes from the river of the same name and means 'White Water'. It was made a burgh in the reign of Alexander II (1214–49) and thereafter developed as a highly successful trade centre with a thriving sea port. In 1372 it was further elevated to a king's burgh by Robert II and thus gained equal status with Ayr which had been made a royal burgh some time between 1202 and 1206.

For a long time Irvine was the sole port for the City of Glasgow, but as Glasgow itself developed, Irvine became insufficient for its needs and in 1668 the Glasgow burgesses purchased land further up the Clyde Estuary and built Port

Glasgow. As Glasgow became increasingly important as an international trading centre during the eighteenth century, Irvine once again became Glasgow's main port, and for a short time during this century it was the third largest port in Scotland. In 1768 an English engineer, John Golborne, devised a method of narrowing and deepening the Clyde, thus making it navigable as far as Glasgow itself. This had a devastating effect on Irvine. Until the end of the nineteenth century the port was principally used for the export of coal, but in the twentieth century this trade declined, and by the 1950s had ended. By the beginning of the twentieth century the population had fallen to just 10,000, but once it was developed as a new town Irvine regained its position as one of Strathclyde Region's largest towns, with a population of 55,850. The town's Scottish Maritime Museum, Magnum Centre and Glasgow Vennel are all worth visiting. The latter is a street which was the main road to Glasgow from the fifteenth century until the end of the seventeenth century. It was designated a conservation area by the Irvine Development Corporation in 1974 and since then there has been a major programme of restoration to the eighteenth and nineteenth-century buildings

Glasgow Vennel, Irvine

109

and street. The overall effect, seen today, is a fine example of a completely restored street which recaptures the atmosphere of two centuries ago. The Vennel is of great historical importance to Irvine. Here, for instance, is where Robert Burns came to live and work in 1781. He intended to set up in partnership with his mother's half-brother Alexander Peacock at the heckling shop, learning the flax-dressing trade as he went along. He lodged in a tiny, damp attic room just a few doors up from the heckling shop. During his ten-month stay in Irvine he suffered from frequent bouts of ill-health and depression. Later the shop caught fire, thus ending the partnership and forcing Burns to return home to the family farm near Tarbolton. The heckling shop is now situated behind the Glasgow Vennel Museum and is well worth a visit. It is also possible to visit Burns's lodgings by arrangement with the museum staff.

The cycleway is clearly defined from Kilwinning to Irvine, coming to an end at the Beach Park. Back once more to Howgate, Irvine and the route for Ardrossan. Here it follows minor roads for two miles until it enters Ardeer Park. The cycleway follows the coastal promenade for most of the next two and a half miles through Stevenston, Saltcoats and finally to where it ends at Ardrossan. These towns, although having distinctly separate identities, are now physically joined together. They are all ancient towns, Ardrossan and Stevenston both having castles built by Anglo–Norman knights on land given to them by Hugh de Morville in the twelfth century. Kerelaw Castle in Stevenston was probably built by Simon de Beaumont. Later it came into the hands of the Cunninghames of Glencairn who had a long-running feud with their prominent neighbours, the Montgomeries of Eglinton, who in the seventeenth century sacked and burned the castle, leaving it a ruin.

The castle in Ardrossan was built by Arthur of Ardrossan, an indigenous Celtic knight who vowed homage to King David I and was therefore able to stay on the land he had held already. The castle was held by many families before it was taken over by the Montgomeries of Eglinton in 1484, and destroyed by Cromwell's troops in 1648.

This area was once a great centre for coalmining and Stevenston was where the shaft of the first deep pit was sunk in 1678. This pit was called Deep Shank Pit. On Auchenharvie golf course adjacent to the foreshore is the ruin of Beam Engine House which, as its name suggests, housed a large engine which was installed in 1719 to drive the pumping system which kept the coal workings beneath dry.

Saltcoats was made a burgh of barony in 1528 by James V. The name Saltcoats or Saltcottis simply means 'saltworkers' cottages' and, of course, the salt pans provided the first industry of the town by extracting salt from sea-water. It was also the first place in Britain to manufacture magnesium sulphate (more commonly known as Epsom Salts). The town became a centre for shipbuilding, fishing and weaving, and its harbour was used for the transportation of coal – but it was also infamously known as a centre for smugglers. Later, in the latter part of the nineteenth and the first half of the twentieth centuries, Saltcoats became a very popular holiday resort, particularly with Glaswegians. As a child, my mother used to spend all her summer holidays in Saltcoats. Since the advent of the foreign package holiday, however, Saltcoats along with many other Scottish holiday resorts has suffered a decline in popularity.

The traveller passes from Saltcoats into Ardrossan by way of Burns Road to South Crescent Road, then past Arran Road and Princes Street, turning left into Harbour Road, reaching Ardrossan Harbour and the end of the cycleway. The harbour, once a busy transatlantic port, was also the railway terminus for passengers boarding ships for ferries to Ireland, the Isle of Man and Arran. Now, alas, the only ferry service still running is the car ferry, *The Isle of Arran*, which sails between Ardrossan and Brodick.

Arran still enjoys a thriving tourist trade and quite deservedly, for in my view it is one of the most beautiful islands in Scotland. It offers tourists everything they could possibly want in an outdoor holiday – it is 'Scotland in miniature', with high mountains, charming villages, sandy beaches, rocky bays and woodland areas, and, of course, the opportunity for unrestricted

111

walking, climbing and cycling. Arran is also the gateway to the Highlands with its other ferry from Lochranza to Claonaig (summer only).

CHAPTER 10

The Johnstone to Greenock and Largs Cycleway

This cycleway parts from the Glasgow to Irvine Cycleway at the first footbridge the traveller comes to which crosses the Johnstone–Howwood bypass. Simply cross the bridge for Greenock or keep straight on past this footbridge for Irvine. This route also follows the disused Glasgow to Greenock (Prince's Pier) railway line, built in the 1860s. The route is clearly defined until it reaches Kilmacolm, so there is no need to describe it in detail.

After three-and-a-half miles of mostly wooded railway cutting, the traveller comes to Bridge of Weir. It was the railway which brought many new inhabitants to Bridge of Weir in the nineteenth century, with professional people whose business was in Glasgow or Paisley moving to a more rural setting. The village today is still an extremely pleasant place. It has one historic building, Ranfurly Castle, located on the Bridge of Weir to Howwood road. It was built by the Knox family in 1440 who occupied it until the beginning of the eighteenth century, but it is now derelict.

It is four miles from the village to Kilmacolm; look out for the group of sculptures by artist David Kemp on the way. On this

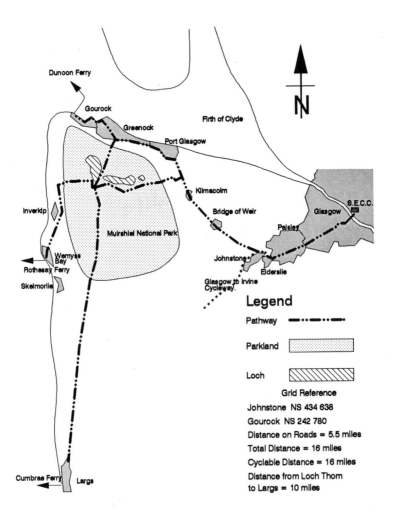

Dunoon Ferry

Gourock

Greenock

Port Glasgow

Firth of Clyde

N

Kilmacolm

Bridge of Weir

Glasgow

S.E.C.C.

Inverkip

Paisley

Muirshiel National Park

Wemyss Bay

Johnstone

Elderslie

Rothesay Ferry

Skelmorlie

Glasgow to Irvine Cycleway.

Legend

Pathway ●—●●—●●—●●—●

Parkland

Loch

Grid Reference

Johnstone NS 434 638

Gourock NS 242 780

Distance on Roads = 5.5 miles

Total Distance = 16 miles

Cyclable Distance = 16 miles

Distance from Loch Thom to Largs = 10 miles

Cumbrae Ferry Largs

A Roman legion on the Johnstone to Greenock cycleway, by sculptor David Kemp

stretch of the route can be seen a series of buildings some quarter of a mile away to the west. These are the Quarrier's Village for orphan children. The founder was William Quarrier who was born in Greenock in 1829. A successful businessman, he started looking after orphans from small back-street premises in Glasgow. In 1876 he bought Nittingshill Farm, where he started building the village that is still in use today. Two years later he moved 180 children from the squalor of Glasgow into the first ten cottages to be finished, in this new beautiful environment, where for the first time the children could lead a healthy life. Many more cottages were built and many more children soon arrived. By the time Quarrier died in 1903, he was internationally known for his work with orphans.

The village of Kilmacolm is said to have taken its name from St Columba, who established the religious settlement on Iona, one of the most important foundations of the early Christian Church in Scotland. There is no evidence that he ever visited Kilmacolm, however; the settlement was probably called after him by monks from Paisley or Kilwinning.

115

Like its neighbour, Bridge of Weir, Kilmacolm remained a tiny hamlet until it was opened up by the railway. The town has many beautiful buildings by some of the most notable architects of the time. Of special note are Rowantree Hill designed by James Salmon, and Windyhill by Charles Rennie Mackintosh.

Within Kilmacolm, the traveller comes to the Pullman Restaurant and Bar which now occupies Kilmacolm Railway Station building, and from here on the route needs a little explanation. Pass this bar (or stop for a drink – it's a nice place for some refreshment. Children are fully catered for, and under the adjacent railway bridge is a bicycle rack). Continue straight on into a piece of waste ground. From here take a path on the left which, within a few metres, enters a small housing estate. Turn right into Whitelee Crescent and go to the end of the road, where the cycleway recommences and continues for a further one and a half miles to where the railway path ends. Here turn left on to a minor road and climb up to the bridge which you have just passed under on the cycle track. Cross this bridge and turn right on to another minor road, Auchenbothie Road (these instructions are for cyclists because walkers can still use the railway, this rough path being perfectly suitable for walking).

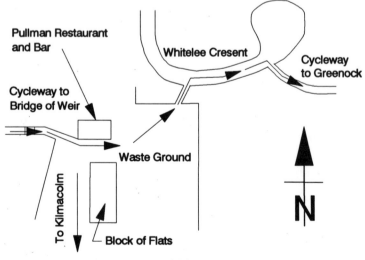

116

At this point it is worth mentioning that the spot where the cycleway leaves the railway is an excellent place to head for the hills. Instead of turning left to go over the bridge, carry straight on in the opposite direction, taking care to keep on the correct road – this is an area with many small unclassified roads going off in all directions. The correct route is as follows: at the first junction, bear right; at the second T-junction, turn right; at the third junction, turn left. After about a mile and a half this unclassified road joins the B788 Greenock to Kilmacolm road. Here turn left and, within a very short distance on the opposite side of the B788, there is another unclassified road. Follow this road which will take the traveller deep into the countryside (cyclists should take care as this road deteriorates into a very rough track in places – only mountain bikes are suitable). It goes past the Gryffe Reservoirs and Loch Thom, where travellers have three options: either to go down to Greenock via Whinhill, Inverkip; or to go due south for nine miles along the old Greenock to Largs road (for cyclists this must be one of the most direct and safe routes from Paisley to Largs).

The Port Glasgow and Greenock area, now part of the 30,000-acre Muirshiel Regional Park, has much to offer the visitor. On the moorland road from Greenock to Inverkip is the Cornalees Bridge Centre, which houses the rangers' office, toilets

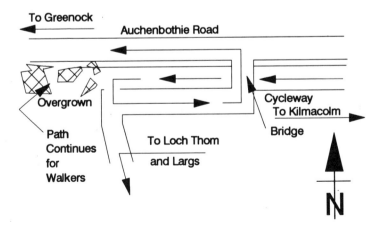

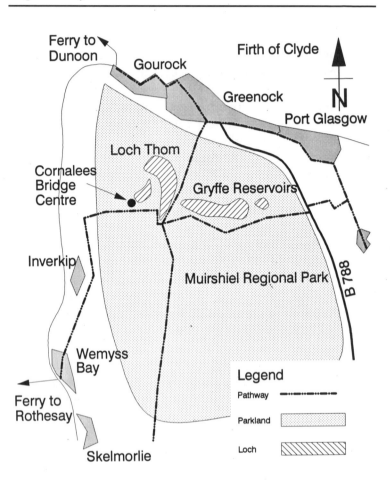

and a visual display about the area. From there are many country walks including the trail which follows the banks of Greenock Cut, the aqueduct taking Greenock's water supply from Loch Thom through filters to Overton, the compensating dam below. Loch Thom is really a man-made dam, built in the 1830s and called after the civil engineer Robert Thom who had surveyed the area some years before.

Return to Auchenbothie Road, and carry on for almost two miles to a housing estate called Bardainney. Turn first left into Montrose Avenue and follow this road till it joins Dubbs Road.

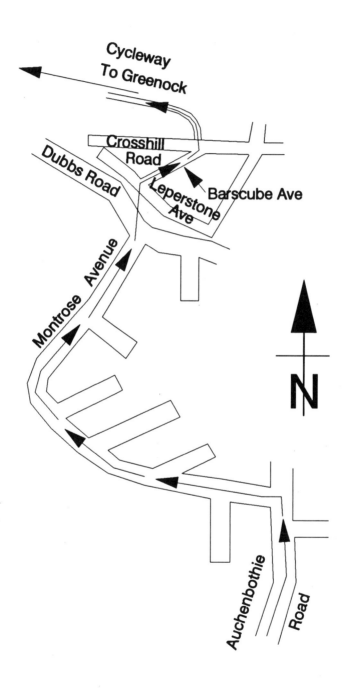

Cycleway
To Greenock

Crosshill
Road

Dubbs Road

Leperstone
Ave

Barscube Ave

Montrose Avenue

N

Auchenbothie

Road

Cross and pass the deterrent poles which separate Dubbs Road from Leperstone Avenue. Go left by way of Barscube Avenue as it sweeps over a small rise down to Crosshill Road where the cycleway resumes on the railway path just to the left of the social club. It follows the southern boundary of Port Glasgow into the heart of Greenock.

Greenock and Port Glasgow grew up during the Industrial Revolution. Port Glasgow was built on land purchased for the city of Glasgow in 1668 to become the port for this fast expanding city and was known as Newport Glasgow (the 'New' was later dropped from the name). The town's Newark Castle, on the banks of the Clyde, was built by the powerful Maxwell family in 1599. Like so many of the great families of the time, they seemed to indulge themselves in feuds with their neighbours and even other branches of their own family. Patrick Maxwell, the builder of Newark Castle, who was made a Justice of the Peace in 1623, was said to have killed at least two of his neighbours. These were Hugh, the fourth Earl of Eglinton (although this murder is also attributed to one of the Cunninghame family), and Patrick Maxwell of Staneley. Much of Newark Castle is still intact and is a fine example of a tower-house with barmkin (or courtyard).

On one side of the castle is Newark Castle Park which was built by Inverclyde District Council on reclaimed industrial land, and allows the traveller a direct link to Finlaystone Estate. Now a country park, the estate was the seat of the Earls of Glencairn since the fifteenth century. The eighteenth-century house is now the home of the chief of the Clan MacMillan and is open to the public by appointment on summer weekends.

On the other side of Newark Castle is the Ferguson Shipyard, alas now the only working yard in this area. Today it specialises in the construction of smaller vessels such as car ferries. Since its earliest days and up to the end of the last decade, Port Glasgow had been a major centre for shipbuilding, pioneering many new techniques in the industry. In 1812 John Wood constructed the *Comet*, the first steam ship to be built in Europe, adapting the engine from the original steam engine invented by Greenock's James Watt. The *Comet*, which took passengers from Glasgow to Helensburgh and Greenock, can still be seen on the north side of Port Glasgow town centre in Coronation Park.

Greenock has an ancient past; its situation in a sheltered bay would have been an ideal place for prehistoric man to settle. Pottery dating from 1000BC has been found in the area. The Romans, too, had many fortifications in the area and Greenock, as a safe anchorage, might have been where legionaries were ferried across to commence a period of guard duty on the Antonine Wall. The town, whose name means 'sunny place', became a burgh in 1635. Its roots were firmly fixed in all facets of the marine industry, with the town becoming more and more important as a port and then as a centre for shipbuilding. In the seventeenth century it had a thriving herring trade with the German Baltic states and France. The town grew rapidly in the Industrial Revolution with its population increasing five-fold in just 50 years. The growth in transatlantic trade led to a rapid expansion of the harbour and a further development of the shipbuilding industry.

James Watt was born in Greenock in 1736. Although he did not conceive of steam power, he solved the problems of harnessing this power and developed the first high-pressure steam engine, which he patented in 1769. Although his engines were used in both the mining and the cotton industries, Watt was very sceptical about his invention ever being used in ships, and it was only when his patent ran out in the first years of the nineteenth century, that others had the opportunity to develop his design.

During the Second World War Greenock, an important strategic centre, was badly bombed. On 6 May 1940, between 250 and 300 German bombers attacked the town in three waves. The devastating attack lasted three hours with 280 people being killed and 1,200 others injured. Half of the 18,000 houses in the town were damaged, with over 1,000 of these being destroyed completely. Much of Greenock's industry lay in ruins. Walker's and Westburn sugar refineries suffered direct hits and the fires were said to have burned with such intensity that molten sugar ran in rivers down the streets towards the Clyde. Later, once this sugar had cooled and solidified, it was broken out and re-used.

Part of the town centre has been declared a conservation area and many buildings from the eighteenth and nineteenth centuries are being given a major face-lift. These include the Municipal Buildings and spectacular Victoria Tower, and the Customs House designed by William Burn and built in 1818, which is still used by the Customs and Excise today. Close by is Customs House Quay where many Scottish emigrants in the last century embarked on ships bound for Canada, the USA and Australia.

Travelling west, high above the town on Lyle Hill, is a memorial in the form of a Cross of Lorraine erected in honour of the Free French Forces stationed in Greenock during the Second World War. This spot has one of the most beautiful views over the Firth of Clyde and far beyond.

From Greenock it is only a mile and a half along the coast to Gourock where the traveller can catch the ferry for Dunoon. Gourock, a small fishing port till the end of the last century, became popular as a holiday resort but, as with many towns on the Firth of Clyde, fell from favour in the 1950s.

Going back to Cornalees Bridge Centre, if you follow the road which runs alongside the Greenock Cut and then left just past Majeston, this small unclassified road can be followed past Inverkip to Wemyss Bay where ferries sail for Rothesay on the Isle of Bute.

Now on to Largs by way of the old Greenock to Largs road. Like all those described in this chapter, this is an unclassified road used by very few cars – cyclists and pedestrians should not encounter any problems on it. From the Cornalees Bridge the nine-mile route climbs for about three miles and then descends to Largs.

Largs is a thriving holiday resort, especially popular with day-trippers from many towns and cities in Central Scotland and beyond. Travelling through the town from north to south along the bustling promenade you will first pass the pier, where the ferry to Millport sails continuously back and forward, then the beautiful gardens and the town's museum housed in a Benedictine monastery. Half-a-mile further on is a monument called the Pencil which commemorates the Battle of Largs. The town's association with the Vikings is marked each year by a week of festivities followed by a re-enactment of the Battle of Largs and the burning of a longship. This used to be held on the anniversary of the battle (which took place on 1 October 1263) but it was moved to the summer months so that tourists could join in the celebrations of the Vikings' defeat.

The story of the Battle of Largs, like so much of Scotland's history, has some connection with David I. When the king brought his Anglo-Norman followers to take over the estates of Central Scotland and create a feudal society, many of the indigenous Celtic chiefs had to move to the peripheral areas to escape the jurisdiction of the new order. The Celtic chieftains in areas such as Galloway, Argyll, Moray and Caithness enjoyed a great deal of independence and were in a constant state of conflict with the King of Scotland. Indeed, they owed their allegiance to the King of Norway to whom many were in some way related, and with whom the Lords of the Isles had a treaty. So when one of David's successors, the young King Alexander III, commenced territorial raids against the Hebrides in the summer of 1263, King Hakkon of Norway decided to retaliate. In July he sailed with 150 longships from Norway to Kirkwall where he had hoped to gather more support – but this was not to be. The Norwegians left Kirkwall in August and sailed down the west coast of Scotland. As they entered the Firth of Clyde and dropped anchor in Lamlash Bay to make final preparations for battle, Alexander's army marched to the Royal Burgh of Ayr. He then sent a party of Dominican monks to discuss terms for peace. These were stalling tactics – the King of Scots was waiting for the first autumn storms which would play havoc with the Norwegian fleet.

This was exactly what happened. As the invaders moved to attack, a terrible storm broke and much of the fleet was either destroyed at sea or washed ashore on the coast of Cunninghame close to Largs. The Norwegians, who had not been able to amass in any significant numbers, were quickly repelled by small groups of advanced guard sent quickly from the main advancing Scottish army. When Hakkon saw this army assembling on the hills above Largs, he ordered what was left of his fleet back to Arran where they hastily prepared to sail for home. Back in Kirkwall in December King Hakkon died. Three years later his son, King Magnus, returned the Hebrides to the King of Scotland.

Further out of the town in the same direction is Kelburn Country Centre. This is the estate of the Earl of Glasgow and, indeed, the tenth Earl and Countess still live there. The castle, some of which dates from the thirteenth century, is therefore not open to the public. Kelburn has some fine walks through woods and gorges. It also has very fine views across the Firth of Clyde.

From here on it is only possible to continue the journey by using the footpath of the A78. The footpath is more or less complete all the way to Ardrossan, but this is a very busy main road.

CHAPTER 11

The Glasgow to East Kilbride and Blantyre Cycleway

There are plans to create a walkway along the length of the White Cart River within Paisley and the city of Glasgow. At the moment a series of short distance walkways do exist along its banks in certain areas. This chapter will try to link these walkways together by describing the shortest way possible through the adjoining city streets. It will also entail a tour of some of Glasgow's many southern parks.

Please refer to the last chapter for the first part of the walkway, namely the section of the Glasgow to Irvine Cycleway through Rosshall Park and Crookston to Hawkhead. This is followed by a stretch through Pollok Park. The park can be reached from Bell's Bridge via Bellahouston Park, as also described in Chapter 10. Once in Bellahouston Park, take the perimeter path to the left and leave it again by the gate closest to the junction of Mosspark Boulevard and Dumbreck Road. Cross this junction and continue along Dumbreck Road some 200m to Dumbreck roundabout and turn right into the access road which is shared by Haggs Castle Golf Club and Pollok Park. The entrance to the park is located at the far end of this access road.

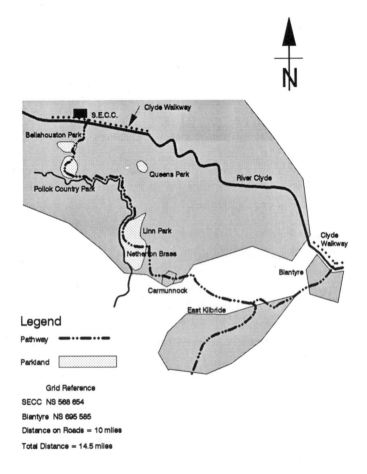

N

Clyde Walkway

S.E.C.C.

Bellahouston Park

Pollok Country Park

Queens Park

River Clyde

Linn Park

Netherton Braes

Clyde Walkway

Carmunnock

Blantyre

East Kilbride

Legend

Pathway

Parkland

Grid Reference

SECC NS 568 654

Blantyre NS 695 585

Distance on Roads = 10 miles

Total Distance = 14.5 miles

Once in Pollok Country Park there are 361 acres of beautiful countryside and woodland, as well as the Burrell Collection and Pollok House to explore. Built in 1983, the Burrell contains close to 8,000 exhibits, some of which are in storage, for although the museum is large, the collection is too extensive for all of it to be on display at once. The collection was gifted to the city by Sir William Burrell, a shipping magnate whose vessels brought these artifacts back to Scotland from all over the world. Within this collection are ceramics, pottery, sculptures, wall hangings, and paintings. He even collected windows and stonework from buildings.

The area that Pollok Country Park now occupies was once Pollok Estate which, until it was presented to the city in 1967, belonged to the Maxwell family who had been on this land for 700 years. Traces can be seen of early settlements such as a medieval earthwork castle with its ditched and banked enclosure known as a ring work, similar to that built not far away at Crookston. The third and present Pollok House was built in 1752, but it differed greatly from how it looks today. It was originally designed in a plain box-style, with the additional wings, terraces, entrance hall, and service area (all of which were designed by Sir Robert Rowand Anderson) being added between 1890 and 1908. During the First World War the house was used as an auxiliary hospital and wards were set up in the dining and billiard rooms.

The park should be left by the main entrance/exit to Pollokshaws Road. There is then a stretch of walkway through Auldhouse Park, though if the traveller is trying to head in a south-easterly direction it is not worth the detour for so short a distance.

At Pollokshaws Road, cross to where the walkway starts between the river and a block of high flats. This is known as Riverbank Street and it finishes at Riverford Road. Turn left here, then turn right to Riverford Road, left to Auldhouse Road, left to Kilmarnock Road, right to Holmbank Avenue which leads on to Tantallon Road, and on to the junction of Millbrae Road. This is a good place to deviate from the route temporarily; if the traveller

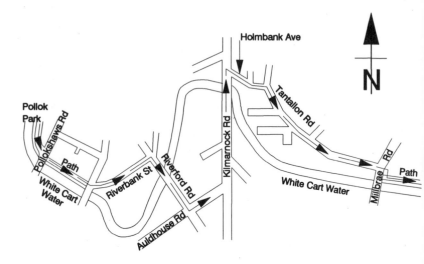

turns left and walks to the end of Millbrae Road, he or she will
come out at Langside Cross where the column commemorating
the Battle of Langside is situated. Here too, on the other side of
Langside Road, access to Queen's Park can be gained.

The whole area from the Cart to Queen's Park was the scene
of the Battle of Langside, which was sparked off by the marriage
of Mary Queen of Scots to the Earl of Bothwell, an action which
turned the Scots people against their queen. She was imprisoned
and her infant son was crowned King James VI; Mary's half-
brother, Lord James Stewart, was appointed regent. Mary
escaped but was pursued by the regent's army, who caught up
with her and her forces at Langside. The regent's army held the
high ground which is now part of Queen's Park, while Mary's
forces, commanded by the fifth Earl of Argyll, were situated on
Clincart Hill where Langside College stands today. The battle
itself, a very fierce and well-matched struggle, was a short affair
lasting only three-quarters of an hour. It ended as a hand-to-hand
brawl, with soldiers using stones and broken pikes as cudgels.
The regent had the advantage of snipers who, hiding behind
walls, were able to fire into the mass of the queen's forces. The
deciding factor, however, was the reinforcements brought in on
the regent's side. The queen's men then began to break and run,

with the other side in hot pursuit. The queen is said to have been watching the battle from Court Knowe, which is now in Linn Park. This is unlikely, however, because of its close proximity to Cathcart Castle which was in the hands of her enemies. Her entourage is more likely to have kept on the move along the high ground between Carmunnock and Kirk hillock from where a good view of the battle could be had. When eventually she saw her forces running towards her in disarray she had no alternative but to flee, leaving by the Carmunnock road and heading south to England.

It is interesting to note that villages such as Langside, Cathcart and Carmunnock, which are now so much a part of the city, were considered then to be far enough away to become holiday resorts where eighteenth-century Glaswegians would rent cottages in the summer.

Recommencing along the route, cross Millbrae Road to where the walkway starts again, following the north bank of the Cart to Carmichael Place. From here go by way of Cartside Road to Sinclair Drive, where the walkway links with Cartside Quadrant and Spean Street, till the junction with Holmlea Road. Cross this and go on into Old Castle Road, then right at Netherlee Road.

This is the site of the old village of Cathcart with many of the original buildings still standing. One can see clearly the layout of this village even though, as with Langside, it has been taken over by the city. The Snuff Mill Bridge across the Cart was built in 1624 and is still used today. Once it carried the mail coach from Glasgow south by way of the Mearns to Kilmarnock. Next to the bridge is Snuff Mill, a seventeenth-century corn mill, converted to paper-making in 1812, and now redeveloped as flats.

As Netherlee Road sweeps left into Greenock Avenue, on the right is an entrance to Linn Park which was once part of an estate called Hagtonhill, owned by the Maxwells of Pollok. It was acquired by a Glasgow businessman in 1820, who set about building the mansion house which is used today as the base for the countryside ranger service, with a nature room and a pets' corner for children at the rear. This estate changed hands many times, once even being bought by the Earl of Cathcart. Glasgow Corporation purchased the estate for the city in 1919 and set aside 212 acres for the park and the adjacent 18-hole golf course. The River Cart runs from north to south through this long, narrow well-wooded park. The traveller can enter from either side of the river as there is a path on both banks. From Greenock Avenue, the path follows the west bank and the path on the other bank is reached by crossing Snuff Mill Bridge. Only the west bank is in any way suitable for cycling, albeit with difficulty. An alternative route for cyclists, avoiding Linn Park, is to continue along Old Castle Road until the junction with Simshill Road. Here turn right and then take the footpath on the right after about 200m or so. This footpath leads on to Drakemire Drive; turn left and continue to the junction with Lainshaw Drive. At this point the cycleway rejoins the route explained in the following paragraphs. In order to get to the hill above the west bank of the river, turn right from Greenock Avenue back on to Old Castle Road. The path into this area of the park starts about 50m on the left.

The path on the east bank is a very pleasant woodland walk which carries on for more than two miles. After a mile or so it passes a bridge (which, after spanning the river, leads to the south end of the park) and finishes at Alyth Gardens in Netherlee.

To get to Clarkston Toll or Busby from here, turn left from Alyth Gardens to Monteith Drive, right into Stamperland Gardens, right into Moray Drive and right into Strawhill Road at the end of which is Busby Road, with East Kilbride to the right and Clarkston Toll a short distance to the left.

The path, which commences along the west bank of the river, goes through the park itself and it is from here that the mansion house is reached. It is also from this side of the river that the way continues. At the south end of the park there is a grassy common which sweeps up a hill to a children's play area. At the top of this hill is what the local people call 'The Gap' – a large gap in the fence leading to the grounds of Linn Crematorium. Go this way (keeping a respectful distance from the crematorium) and leave by the gate at the bottom of the hill. On the opposite side of this

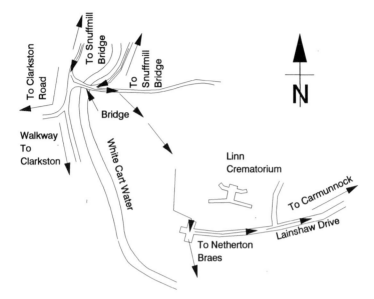

road is Linn Cemetery and from here access to Netherton Braes, designated a site of scientific interest, can be gained. No bicycles are allowed in this area.

Turn left at the crematorium gates into Lainshaw Drive and continue to the top of the hill. Turn right into Holmbyre Road, at the end of which a little path should be climbed up to Carmunnock Road where there is a roundabout. This is now the south-eastern extremity of Castlemilk. Continue over this roundabout staying on Carmunnock Road to the village of Carmunnock itself. Carmunnock is still a complete and very picturesque village which is now within Glasgow. This village has been in existence since the Dark Ages when St Cadoc, sent north from Wales in 528AD to convert the local Celtic communities to Christianity, founded a church here. The name is said to come from the Brythonic Gaelic words *cear mynoc* meaning 'the monk's fort'. This Christian settlement became part of the Diocese of Paisley Abbey in the thirteenth century, and was administered by monks sent from there who also taught the local inhabitants how to farm.

In the early part of the nineteenth century this area was the haunt of body-snatchers and a gatehouse had to be built in Carmunnock churchyard for the guards posted to watch for any signs of this barbaric activity. There is a board still hanging in the gatehouse today, detailing the orders for the watch as follows:

> There are two on Watch each night, who are to go on an hour after sunset and continue till after daybreak in winter and after sunrise in summer. They are strictly prohibited from getting intoxicated or leaving the churchyard during that time, and no visitor is allowed to enter on any account without giving the password for the night. They are also prohibited from firing guns, except when there is cause of alarm that any of the inhabitants in such cases may be able to turn out to the assistance of the Watch. Any damage that may be done to the Watchhouse or to the furnishings is to be repaired at the expense of those who make it.
>
> Ordered at Carmunnock on 8 Jan 1828

Carmunnock suffered a constant increase in traffic volume in the early twentieth century because it was on the main Glasgow to East Kilbride road. This problem worsened dramatically from the 1950s when the new town of East Kilbride was being developed and Castlemilk housing estate was built close by. The problem became so bad that it was thought some of the oldest cottages in the village would have to be demolished due to structural problems caused by heavy vehicles using the adjacent roads. In 1988, however, the Carmunnock Bypass was opened, alleviating the traffic problems and allowing Carmunnock to regain its village character.

From Carmunnock, take the B759 Cathkin road which goes back towards the east side of Glasgow. (Incidentally, if the traveller continues along the B759 for two miles, Cathkin Braes is reached. This is another area of country park and, at 600ft above sea-level, is the highest park in Glasgow.) Take the first road on the right, signposted to Rogerton. This is a very quiet unclassified road which should cause no problems for pedestrians or cyclists (as indeed no particular difficulty should be experi-

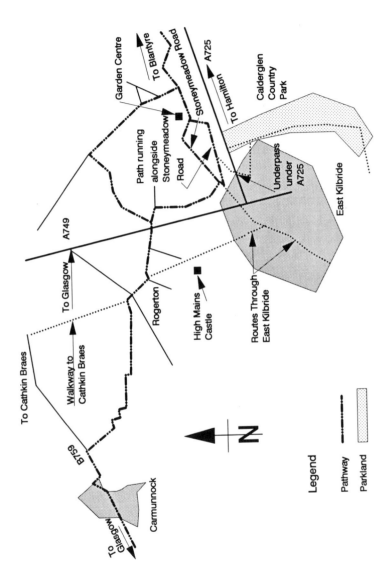

Legend

Pathway

Parkland

N

To Cathkin Braes

To Glasgow

Walkway to Cathkin Braes

B759

Carmunnock

To Glasgow

Rogerton

High Mains Castle

A749

To Glasgow

Routes Through East Kilbride

East Kilbride

Underpass under A725

Path running alongside Stoneymeadow Road

Garden Centre

To Blantyre

Stoneymeadow Road

A725

To Hamilton

Calderglen Country Park

enced on any road thus far described). From Rogerton the traveller can get to East Kilbride by turning right and following this road past High Mains and Leigh Mains, coming into East Kilbride at Stewartfield. This is described fully in the next chapter, as is a cycle route to Strathaven via East Kilbride.

At High Mains, the ruins of Mains Castle can be found. It was built by Roger de Valoins, one of the many Anglo–Norman knights to come to Scotland with David I. The castle and estate were taken over by the Comyn family in the early part of the century when David Comyn married Isabella de Valoins. The estate remained in their hands until confiscated by Robert the Bruce a century later. When Bruce's daughter Marjory married Walter Fitzalan, the High Steward of Scotland, the estate was given as part of her dowry. This marriage was to found the Stewart dynasty when the son of Fitzalan and Marjory Bruce became King Robert II on the death of David II, Bruce's son, in 1371.

Mains Castle was given to John Lindsay as part of the Barony of Kilbride by the High Steward of Scotland in 1382 and was confirmed by royal charter of Robert II. The castle was occupied by the Lindsay family till it was sold to the Stuarts of Castlemilk in 1619 to help repay the massive debts incurred by Alexander Lindsay, a cruel and callous man who squandered away the family fortune and died in a state of penury. Legend has it, while curling on a frozen loch on the estate one day, Alexander accused one of his opponents, a tenant by the name of Crawford, of cheating. He ordered a hole to be made in the ice and the unfortunate Crawford was pushed through and left to drown in the ice-cold water. From then on the castle fell into disrepair. First it was used by the Stuarts as a dovecot and then it was left totally empty until 1790 when it was partly demolished and the stone taken to build Torrance House at Calderglen (now the centrepiece of Calderglen Country Park). Today the tower of Mains Castle has been restored and may soon be opened to the public.

If the traveller wishes to go to Blantyre then carry straight on to the junction of the A749 Glasgow to East Kilbride road. Cross this road and take a series of unclassified roads past Nerston. Then turn right and right again past Letrickhills Farm, keeping to the right past two further junctions. Finally turn left into Stoneymeadow Road. An alternative after the East Kilbride road is to go via Chapelside Road, which means turning first right before reaching Nerston. This road is the access road to East Kilbride Golf Club and actually passes through their carpark before continuing down to join Stoneymeadow Road opposite Whin Place. Stoneymeadow Road is the old road from East Kilbride to Blantyre and, since the East Kilbride Expressway was built, it is now very quiet.

After being on this road for about half a mile, the traveller comes to the entrance to Greenhall Park. Once inside, follow the main wooded avenue through the park until it comes to a clearing. Here take the path down through the gorge to the banks of the Rotten Calder, cross a footbridge, turn right and follow the path as it continues along the north bank of the river, passing under a disused railway viaduct. Continue along this path, climbing four stiles, and then cross the river again at another footbridge. Once across this bridge the path crosses a recreational area and continues up a steep hill (known locally as the Pech Brae) and out on to Hunthill Road, Blantyre. Turn left here and follow this road as it continues straight across a road junction where it becomes Bardykes Road. After a short distance turn right into Glasgow Road.

In the thirteenth century a priory was set up on the banks of the Clyde, where Blantyre is now, by a group of Augustinian monks from Jedburgh Abbey. There is a famous legend about their monastery: William Wallace, on escaping from defeat at Glasgow, allegedly sought sanctuary in the monastery – but when his pursuers arrived only minutes later, his only way of escape was by jumping through a window into the Clyde below.

The development of this predominantly rural community – which was probably there a lot earlier than the thirteenth century – only came about with the start of the weaving industry at the beginning of the 1700s. This was followed by cotton-spinning and then by coalmining, and by the middle of the eighteenth century Blantyre had become a sizeable community as a result of the Industrial Revolution.

By the latter part of the nineteenth century coalmining was the predominant industry of the town. In 1877 Blantyre suffered a terrible mining disaster. There were three mining companies with pits in the area, each trying to compete with the others in both output and price. To do this, safety regulations were deliberately ignored and there was a large build-up of gas known as 'firedamp'. At nine o'clock on the morning of Monday, 22 October, a huge explosion occurred underground, killing over two hundred miners. A memorial was erected in 1977 to mark the centenary of this catastrophe.

Follow Glasgow Road to the junction with Station Road, turn right, and at the end of Station Road is the David Livingstone Centre. It is also where the Clyde Walkway is located (see Chapter 1).

CHAPTER 12

Three Shorter Pathways in and around Glasgow

Clyde Pedestrian and Cycle Tunnels and link to the
Glasgow–Irvine Cycleway

As I have researched the various existing cycle routes, some problems have come to light. One is, for instance, the Glasgow section of the Glasgow to Irvine Cycleway. As explained in Chapter 9, this section is at least 60 per cent on roads, and although this in itself is not a bad thing as long as the cyclist doesn't have to share the route with a high volume of traffic, here this is not always possible. Also, although I believe that some day in the future this route will be marked out on the road and some form of traffic management scheme put in place, at present this route is not easy to negotiate.

I would therefore propose the Clyde Tunnel as an alternative for people travelling from the city, although this, too, is not without its problems. The Clyde Tunnel is very long and, for some, a little claustrophobic. In addition, some people might wonder what is 'lurking round the corner'. In my experience there has not been anything lurking round the corner, but I could just have been lucky. I would, therefore, suggest that one should

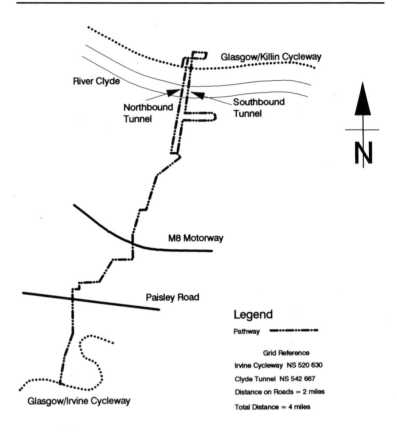

be aware of the situation before attempting any cycle route, especially women and children on their own.

The other problem is that the gradients in the tunnel tend to be fairly steep and it is only the very fit who will emerge not feeling a little out of breath. This is offset, of course, by the fact that it is great fun on the way down. There are two cycle tunnels and a one-way system operates, so you shouldn't encounter any other cyclists coming towards you in the opposite direction. It is the same for pedestrians.

The route is as follows: use the Glasgow–Loch Lomond Cycleway (see Chapter 3) to Whiteinch. Turn right into Smith Street (Smith Street is at the foot of the ramp which leads down from the elevated section of cycleway) and follow this 150m or so

138

to Dumbarton Road. Here turn right along Dumbarton Road for another 150m, going over a ramped section of road. Turn left into Inchholm Street. Follow this round three sides of a block of flats to where the entrance to the cycle tunnel is located. On leaving the tunnel, turn left on to Govan Road where a round-about can be seen. Take the third exit off this roundabout (Skipness Drive). Follow this road as it turns left, passing along-side the eastern carriageway of the main Clyde Tunnel Approach Road in a southerly direction, until the junction of Langlands Road is reached. Continue in the same direction for a short distance to a roundabout under Mossend Flyover. Here take the third exit (Shieldhall Road) but immediately turn on to the foot-path and back around the pedestrian barrier; follow the footpath under Mossend Flyover and continue in a southerly direction alongside the western carriageway of the tunnel approach road. This footpath then crosses the M8 via a footbridge and comes out at Queensland Drive. Turn right, then first left into Ladykirk Drive, and then go by Allanton Road and Dryburn Avenue to Hillington Road. Turn left into Hillington Road, then first right into Tinwauld Avenue and left into Sandwood Road. Cross the busy junction at Paisley Road into Crookston Road where a quarter of a mile on is the bridge over the White Cart and the way into the Irvine Cycleway as described in Chapter 9.

If cycling this route in the opposite direction to that described above, please note the following: at Mossend Flyover, when you turn into Shieldhall Road after coming down the foot-path adjacent to the western carriageway of the tunnel approach road, take the first road on the right (Cowden Street), and from there the way through the tunnel is clearly signposted.

Pollock Shopping Centre to Darnley Mill and Barrhead
At the moment the only way to get from Pollok Park to the Pollok Shopping Centre is to use the pavement of Pollokshaws Road and Barrhead Road, and then by crossing Barrhead Road via the footbridge to enter Pollok Shopping Centre. This route, which can be cycled, starts at the south end of the shopping centre on Cowglen Road. It is a clearly defined footpath which

The 400-year-old sycamore which legend says Mary Queen of Scots once sat under

follows the Brock Burn for about a mile, passing under Kennishead Road and through the Darnley housing estate, and finishing at Nitshill Road at the junction with Kennishead Road. (The huge and very beautiful sycamore tree which can be seen here is, according to legend, the tree that Mary Queen of Scots and Lord Darnley sat under while Mary nursed Darnley back to health after a bout of illness.)

The route goes on by way of Corselet Road. Cross the very busy Nitshill Road at the traffic lights. This area is known as Darnley Mill and Glasgow City Council intends to develop the 100-acre site as a country park. There is also a plan to designate the area around the Brock Burn as 'an area of special scientific interest', similar to that of Netherton Braes. The Darnley Mill area is public land, so there is no reason why people cannot use it for walking. Be careful, of course, to heed any warning or danger signs.

Carry on along Corselet Road for about quarter of a mile to where a footpath forks to the right. Take this footpath and within three-quarters of a mile it joins Aurs Road in Barrhead.

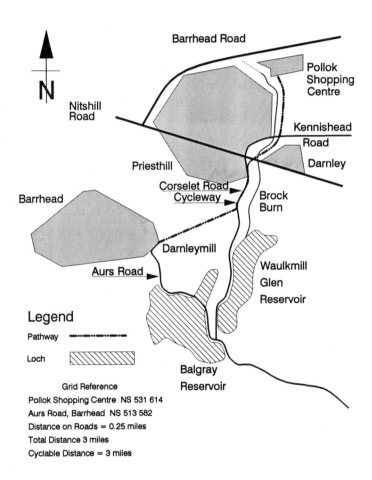

Barrhead Road

Pollok Shopping Centre

Nitshill Road

Kennishead Road

Darnley

Priesthill

Corselet Road Cycleway

Brock Burn

Barrhead

Darnleymill

Waulkmill Glen Reservoir

Aurs Road

Balgray Reservoir

N

Legend

Pathway

Loch

Grid Reference
Pollok Shopping Centre NS 531 614
Aurs Road, Barrhead NS 513 582
Distance on Roads = 0.25 miles
Total Distance 3 miles
Cyclable Distance = 3 miles

Eaglesham to Barrhead

This route is only mentioned in passing as it is on a fairly busy road all the way and it is not ideal for walking, running or cycling. It does, however, serve as the missing link completing a circle which runs via Glasgow, East Kilbride, Darvel, Eaglesham and Barrhead.

Eaglesham is a village with a very long history. It was the original home of the Montgomeries, Anglo–Norman knights, who had been granted land by Walter Fitzalan. In 1360 Sir John de Montgomerie married Elizabeth, the daughter of Sir Hugh de Eglintoune of Ardrossan. When Eglintoune died 20 years later, the baronies of Eglinton and Ardrossan were added to the Montgomeries' estate and the family came to live at Eglinton. There is no trace of their castle left at Eaglesham, for it was considered a ruin even in the eighteenth century.

The village underwent great changes in 1769, when the tenth Earl of Eglinton had the old village demolished and a new, planned village built in its place. This new village was constructed in the form of a letter A and is a striking example of Scottish domestic architecture of the time. The two streets that form the 'A' are Polnoon Street and Montgomerie Street and, with the large common between, the shape is still clearly visible on a map. Today, this extremely pleasant village has been listed as a site of architectural and historical interest. It has become a conservation area and most of the village's buildings have been refurbished, their original thatched roofs all now replaced by slate.

Leave Eaglesham by the B767 to Busby. At the edge of the town the Humbie Road to Newton Mearns starts on the left. Take this road, which comes out at Mearns Cross.

Like Eaglesham, Newton Mearns is now a residential area, though a village has existed here since medieval times. Its first church was built as early as 1178. Mearns Castle, the ruins of which can still be seen today, dates from the beginning of the fourteenth century. Alas there is nothing left of the ancient village, the Revd George McLetchie writing in 1796 that 'the only antique left here in Mearns is the castle'.

From Mearns Cross go straight through the junction with

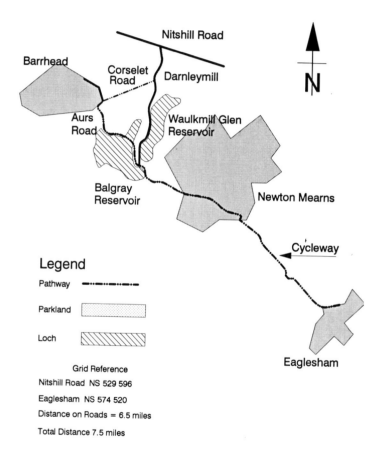

Nitshill Road

Barrhead

Corselet
Road
Darnleymill

N

Aurs
Road

Waulkmill Glen
Reservoir

Balgray
Reservoir

Newton Mearns

Cycleway

Legend

Pathway

Parkland

Loch

Eaglesham

Grid Reference

Nitshill Road NS 529 596

Eaglesham NS 574 520

Distance on Roads = 6.5 miles

Total Distance 7.5 miles

the A77 at the traffic lights and on down to the junction of the B769 Stewarton road. Turn left on to the B769 for 200m or so, and then turn right into Aurs Road. Follow this road around the Balgray Reservoir. (Halfway round the reservoir on the right is the other end of Corselet Road referred to in the previous paragraph. This runs past Ryat Linn Reservoir and Waulkmill Reservoir but apparently there are gates across this road further on, thus allowing no access through to Barrhead Road.) Although, as stated earlier, these are busy roads, this is still by far the least congested of all the routes from Eaglesham to Glasgow.

Turn right and, continuing in Aurs Road, take the first small junction on the right where the path, also referred to in the last paragraph, terminates.

CHAPTER 13

Walkways and Cycleways in and around East Kilbride

When the new town of East Kilbride was first planned back in 1947, it was decided to segregate pedestrians and cyclists from the road system. This decision has proved to be a very good one since, with the vast increase in the volume of traffic using urban areas, East Kilbride ranks as one of the safest urban areas for pedestrians and cyclists in Scotland. It is possible to walk or cycle around most of the town without having to use any of the busy roads.

Since the town as a whole is well served with roads and pathways, I am only going to mention those which join up with longer-distance cycleways in the surrounding district. The many unclassified roads which leave East Kilbride in all directions are all well suited to any of the three activities for which this book has been written. Indeed, it must be said there is no area in Central Scotland better off for this kind of road. It would, therefore, be a pointless exercise to describe all these routes in detail.

From High Mains (described in Chapter 11), continue down Markethill Road to Markethill roundabout. There turn left on to East Mains Road, then take the first right into Old Coach Road.

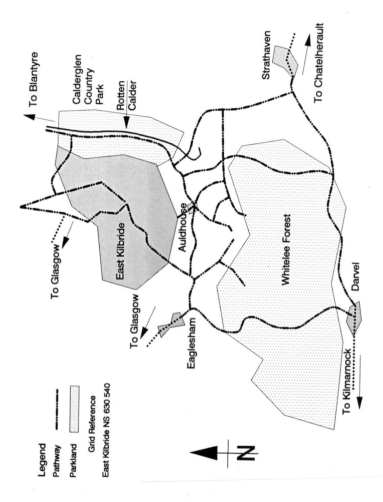

Legend

Pathway

Parkland

Grid Reference

East Kilbride NS 630 540

N

To Blantyre

Calderglen Country Park

Rotten Calder

East Kilbride

To Glasgow

Auldhouse

To Glasgow

Eaglesham

Strathaven

To Chatelherault

Whitelee Forest

Darvel

To Kilmarnock

At the end of this road a cycleway begins which runs parallel to West Mains Road, on through Douglasdale, past West Mains Primary School, across Kirktonholm Road under Queensway, along Lawrence Park and past Westwood Primary School. It then continues across Vancouver Drive around Duncanrig Secondary School, across Westwood Road and through the recreation area, and on to Mossneuk Road. Continue along Mossneuk Road to Wellesley Crescent, carry on along Wellesley Crescent to a footpath off to the left, leading to Eden Grove (which becomes Eden Drive), and left into Greenhills Road. After crossing Newlandsmuir Road, cross over Greenhills Road and go down a ramp into Newlands Road. This is now open countryside. Continuing along this road leads to a signposted junction. From here it is safe cycling for all the family.

This minor road network goes to Auldhouse, Eaglesham and Strathaven (follow the signs for Langlands Golf Course). From the road which goes to Eaglesham, turn left at the junction just after Milhall Farm (turn right for Eaglesham), then next right, and follow the road to Carrot Farm. Here the old drove road begins which leads all the way to Darvel (passing High Alderstocks) via the huge Whitelees Forest. From Darvel it is also possible, by means of another unclassified road, to go directly to Strathaven.

From Stoneymeadow Road (see Chapter 11) there are two alternative routes. The first, for walkers or runners only, is to Strathaven through Calderglen Country Park – cycling is forbidden in Calderglen. If the traveller turns right in the direction of East Kilbride for a short distance (less than a quarter of a mile), there is an unmarked path into the trees. This path winds its way through a wood towards East Kilbride. Within a short distance a clearing is reached where the path splits. The path to the right follows alongside Stoneymeadow Road (this path is also only suitable for walking) as it heads towards East Kilbride and joins Stoneymeadow Road once again at Whin Place adjacent to an electrical sub-station opposite Chapelside Road (see Chapter 11). The path to the left leads quickly to an underpass going under the East Kilbride Expressway and coming out into the Calderwood housing estate. By going left past the three blocks of multistorey flats (called after London theatres) into Bosworth Road which becomes Tewkesbury Road, then left into Barry Road which sweeps round in a semi-circle, and then left again into Kennilworth down behind the Lammermoor Play Centre, the entrance to Calderglen Country Park can be reached at the bottom of a grassy hill.

Calderglen Country Park, which stretches for almost five miles between the East Kilbride Expressway in the north and the A726 East Kilbride–Strathaven road in the south, is a particularly interesting and attractive place. As its name suggests, its woodland trails run along the banks of the Rotten Calder ('Rotten' refers to its colour – *rot* is the old Scots word for 'red' – not to how it smells, and the river is indeed red, a result of minerals in the rocks). It passes through deep gorges, cascading over many waterfalls such as Black Linn, Trough Linn and Torrance Linn, and flowing through areas of broad-leaf decid-uous woodland and evergreens. Before this, however, the river passes the site of several Calderwood castles built through the ages, the first dating from pre-feudal times. Unfortunately, very little is left today of the last castle, built here in the later part of the eighteenth century. This once-imposing structure was in such a state of neglect and disrepair when the estate was bought by the East Kilbride Development Corporation in 1947 that it was decided to demolish it – it was blown up by the army as a training exercise in 1951. Further on is Torrance House. This eighteenth-century manor house was adapted and rebuilt by Archibald Stuart from the much older castle in the same location designed by William Adam. This building was much larger than its predeces-sor so stone from the nearby Mains Castle had to be used in the construction of the new works and the building was completed in 1790. Today Torrance House is used as the visitor centre of the country park and it houses a small history and natural history museum.

Although the nature trails through Calderglen will take you close to the A726 at East Flatt, there is actually no easy way out of the park from there. The best way out is by the main entrance which, after Torrance House, is straight down the main avenue and out on to the Strathaven road. Here turn left along this road for about 300m to Greenhills Road and follow the signs for Langlands Golf Course. At the next road junction carry straight on. (If you turn right this road skirts around to the south of East Kilbride past Auldhouse, as described earlier.) At the next junction the road to Strathaven is signposted.

For the second of the alternative routes from Stoneymeadow Road, turn right into Braeview Place, at the end of which there is a short walkway linking it with the A749. Cross the A749 (thus avoiding the extremely busy Whirlies Roundabout), turn left and carry on along the footpath for approximately 30m to where another footpath goes off to the right. Take this footpath and turn right into Wilson Place. Take the footpath which can be seen leading under East Mains Road. It follows the line of a disused railway track all the way to the ancient village of East Kilbride. Despite being right in the heart of Scotland's sixth-largest town, this charming old village still manages to retain its original character. Most of its buildings date from the seventeenth and eighteenth centuries, though there has been a settlement here since before feudal times. The parish church was built in 1774 on the site of the medieval church of St Bride which gave the town its name. In the churchyard is the mausoleum of the Stuart family of Torrance. The people of this district were staunch believers in the Covenanting cause and many men from East Kilbride parish fought at the Battle of Bothwell Brig (see Chapter 1). The flag they carried into battle was known as 'the Kilbryde Flag', and can still be seen in Glasgow's Kelvingrove Museum and Art Gallery.

Another interesting building in the town is the Montgomery Arms, built as a coaching inn in the seventeenth century. In front of it is the 'Loupin on Stane'. This large rectangular stone with steps up one side was there to help those who had partaken of a drop too much of the cratur get back on their horse.

Close to the village is Long Calderwood Farm, the birthplace of William and John Hunter, who were born in the early part of the eighteenth century, and who both became eminent physicians and anatomists. John became chief surgeon at St George's Hospital in London. During his life he put together a surgical museum, an important collection which was bequeathed to the nation and now forms part of the museum in the Royal College of Surgeons. The Hunterian Museum in Glasgow University was called after his brother William who bequeathed his important collections of books, coins and paintings to the university.

In Brousterhill is Brousterland House, one of the town's oldest houses. Built in 1737, it is a typical example of traditional Scottish architecture with its crow-stepped gables and small windows. It was used as the old parish manse from 1790 to 1897, and the famous local historian David Ure lodged there while he was the assistant minister at the old parish church.

After leaving the disused railway, the route crosses Main Street and then turns left at Parkhall Street to Kittoch Street. Turn right into West Mains Road here and then right again into Kirktonholme Road. The route continues to the edge of Brousterhill, where it climbs up to Harrington Road, turns right into Cunninghame Road to Park Terrace, and through Claverhill Park where the swimming pool is located. Out again at the Edge of Blacklands Road, the route runs alongside Cornwall Street, and continues under the Centre One Roundabout. This area is all within the town centre.

East Kilbride town centre has one of the largest and busiest indoor shopping malls in the country. The outlying industrial areas are home to factories belonging to some of Britain's biggest and most prestigious companies, among them Rolls-Royce and ICI.

The cycleway now continues across and then parallel to Quebec Drive until it joins the other route already described which leads through the remainder of the town.

There are hundreds of miles of safe cycle routes around East Kilbride and, to take full advantage of the opportunities they offer, I would recommend that the cyclist consult the Ordnance Survey Landranger Series sheet 64 (Glasgow).

CHAPTER 14

Strathaven to Kilmarnock Walkway

Strathaven is a small market town which, although it has seen great changes taking place through the years, has managed to hold on to its traditional character. The town is built round a common green and originally would have been a rabbit warren of narrow streets. Only one or two of these still remain, such as Main Street. The area within the vicinity of the town has supported settlements of people for over 2,500 years and, as the physical aspect of the geography shows, the area was on an easy western route north and therefore has always been subject to a lot of visitors from the south, some less welcome than others. The Romans were among the early visitors to the area and one of their military roads ran from Carstairs through Sandford (just to the south of Strathaven) to Loudoun Hill where there was a large garrison. Parts of this road are still in existence today and it is clearly shown on the Ordnance Survey map. In the town the Boo-Backet Bridge (which means 'highly arched) is reckoned by some to have been built in Roman times; it is certainly consistent with the design of the Roman bridge over the South Calder Water at the north end of Strathclyde Park. Others believe this bridge was built much later, probably in feudal times, on the site

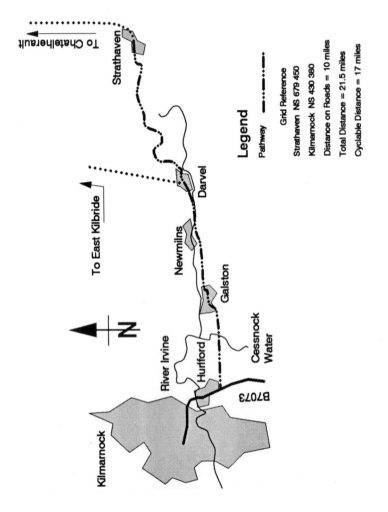

To Chatelherault

Strathaven

To East Kilbride

N

River Irvine

Kilmarnock

Hurtford

Newmilns

Darvel

Galston

Cessnock
Water

B7073

Legend

Pathway — · — · — ·

Grid Reference

Strathaven NS 679 450

Kilmarnock NS 430 380

Distance on Roads = 10 miles

Total Distance = 21.5 miles

Cyclable Distance = 17 miles

of the original Roman bridge.

Not much seems to be known about the family who became the feudal lords of Avendale during the reign of King David I, but the earliest recorded Anglo–Norman family in the area is the Flemings. They passed the lands on to the Baird family, but by the early fifteenth century the area was in the hands – possibly through marriage – of the powerful Douglases. There must have been some form of keep in the area dating from the fourteenth century, which would possibly have stood on the site of the castle that can be seen today. The Earl of Douglas became Regent for the six-year-old James II after King James I was murdered in 1437. Two years later Douglas died and the Regency was passed to Sir William Crichton. Douglas had left two young sons and, fearing the continuing power of the Douglas family, Crichton had the boys summoned to Edinburgh Castle and put to death. The Douglas estates were then divided up and the family's power temporarily weakened.

A title of Lord Avendale was then granted to Andrew Stewart who had a proper castle – five storeys high with many turrets – built in place of the former keep. Stewart would have been the

Strathaven Castle

153

first feudal lord to have actually lived at Strathaven, all previous owners of these lands having resided elsewhere. King James V granted these estates to his loyal supporters the Hamiltons after the Stewarts had sided with the King's enemies – once again, the Douglases. When Oliver Cromwell was in power, Anne the Duchess of Hamilton came to live in Strathaven Castle for a time. She liked the place so much that she returned for short visits throughout the rest of her life. When she died the castle fell into disrepair and was never inhabited again. It is now in such a dangerous state that the public is not allowed near it. One of the legends associated with the castle concerns a particular lord of the castle who was so incensed by his wife's infidelity that he had her bricked up within the cavity of a wall. Later, in the nineteenth century, bones were discovered when part of a wall fell down.

Next to the castle is the town's mill, built by the Duke of Hamilton in 1650 for the local people to have their corn ground. It was used as a mill until 1966, latterly for grinding oatmeal. It was taken over by the town's Arts Guild in the 1970s and refurbished as a theatre and arts complex. There is also a fine museum in the town called the John Hastie Museum, named after a local grocer who, at the end of the nineteenth century, bequeathed a sum of money to build a park and museum for the good of the residents of Strathaven.

The next part of the route goes from Strathaven to Darvel. Start from the street which runs alongside John Hastie Park (Lethame Road), and carry on to the road junction. There turn left, then first right, and this leads on to the unclassified road which goes all the way to Darvel. Just follow the signs.

At the third road junction along the way, it is possible to turn left and follow this road for about a mile until the site of the Battle of Drumclog is reached. It was here on 1 June 1679 that 250 poorly armed Covenanters defeated a troop of the King's Dragoons led by John Graham of Claverhouse. Graham had pursued the Covenanters to Strathaven, reaching the town at six o'clock on that Sunday morning. While at an inn he discovered that there was to be an illegal conventical close to Loudoun Hill. He immediately marched his troops in the direction of Loudoun to intercept the Covenanters. Graham and his men took up what was thought to be a favourable position at the top of a rise, not realising that the ground below them was very boggy. The Covenanters, led by Sir Robert Hamilton, had taken up position on high ground on the other side of the bog and allowed Graham's dragoons to make the attack. They were soon caught deep in the bog where their ranks were broken and confusion ensued. The battle continued with fierce hand-to-hand fighting and ended with the deaths of over 50 loyalists against only three Covenanters. The remainder of the loyalist force, including Graham himself, were forced to flee. He had a narrow escape when he was chased all the way back to Strathaven.

Return to the route where within four miles the small town of Darvel is reached. A couple of miles back along the main road in the direction of Strathaven is Loudoun Hill (316m high). It is a volcanic plug which was scoured by glacial movement into a crag and tail formation. Under this is the site of another battle where, in 1307, William Wallace defeated the English.

Darvel was a planned town built at the beginning of the nineteenth century, which grew from the cotton industry and coalmining. In Hastings Square there is a bust of Alexander Fleming, the famous bacteriologist who was born on a farm just outside the town, and who in 1928 discovered penicillin.

For cyclists, this is the end of the road – or at least the end of the *safe* road, for the only way to Kilmarnock from here is by the main A71. For walkers, however, the way could continue along the dismantled railway – as, indeed, it could have done all the way from Strathaven. This route passes Newmilns and Galston, ending up on the B7073 at Hurlford on the south-eastern outskirts of Kilmarnock. Newmilns became a burgh of barony in 1491 for the Campbell family of Loudoun. Its old townhouse, built in 1739 in the traditional Scottish style with bellcote crownsteps and forestairs, is now the town's information centre. As with Darvel and its westerly neighbour Galston, Newmilns grew with the cotton and coalmining industries.

Just to the north, between Newmilns and Galston, lies the ruins of Loudoun Castle, tragically burned down in 1941. It was first built as a tower house in the sixteenth century and then lavishly turned into a grand mansion in the eighteenth century and was the home of the Campbells, the Earls of Loudoun. In 1647 John Campbell, the first Earl, together with the Earl of Lanark and the Earl of Lauderdale, visited King Charles I when he was imprisoned in Carisbrooke Castle on the Isle of Wight. There they signed the 'Engagement' whereby the Scottish lords promised the king military assistance in return for his agreement to establish presbyterianism in England over a period of three years. Ironically, less than 40 years later, a group of Covenanters was imprisoned in the castle. The local men from Newmilns made a successful rescue attempt, setting the castle on fire as they made their escape.

The route through Galston, from the north-east, is by way of Barrmill Road, then right into Henrietta Street and on into Bridge Street, left into Brewland Street which becomes Ayr Road and, just before the junction of the A719 and the B744, the disused railway recommences on the south-west of the town.

Kilmarnock (which means 'Church of St Marnock') is the biggest town in Ayrshire. In feudal times, the grant of land which

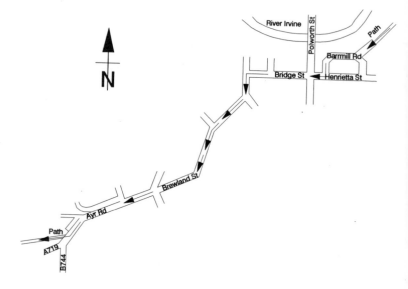

now takes in Kilmarnock was given to Malcolm Loccart. Some time within the next hundred years, possibly through marriage, it was taken over by the Balliol family who later had all their lands confiscated by Robert the Bruce. He gave the lands to Robert Boyd in recognition of his faithful service during the War of Independence. Except for a very short period in the middle of the fifteenth century, the Boyd family possessed these lands for many hundreds of years. They built Dean Castle as a tower house in 1350, adding substantially to it a hundred years later. In 1465 Lord Boyd succeeded Bishop James Kennedy as regent to the 14-year-old King James III, and four years later arranged the marriage of the young king to Margaret, daughter of King Christian I of Norway and Denmark. Margaret brought as her dowry the Orkney and Shetland Islands, which then became part of Scotland. Shortly after this James took over the affairs of state for himself. One of the first things he did was to overthrow Lord Boyd, whom he passionately disliked. Boyd had to flee for his life but returned shortly afterwards to his lands in Kilmarnock.

In September 1562 a covenant to defend the rights of Protestants was signed in Ayr by 78 Ayrshire noblemen, but Lord Boyd of Kilmarnock supported the old faith and later fought for Mary Queen of Scots at the Battle of Langside. The town became a burgh of barony in 1592 under Lord Thomas Boyd.

The fourth Earl of Kilmarnock fought on the side of the Jacobites at Culloden in 1746, although he received no support from either his son or his tenants for this cause. He was captured, taken prisoner and, in 1747, executed for treason at Tower Hill. With his death the earldom ceased.

Some time after this the estate was bought by the Earl of Glencairn who in turn sold it to Henrietta Scott, wife of the Duke of Portland. After she died it was taken over by the eighth Lord Howard de Walden, her nephew. The castle was completely refurbished by him between 1908 and 1936, and when he died in 1946 the castle and its grounds were presented to the town by his son, the ninth Lord Howard de Walden.

Today the castle houses a fine collection of arms and armour, tapestries and early musical instruments. There is also a display

157

on the life and works of Robert Burns. The grounds are now a country park with nature trails and areas of extensive woodlands into which the Fenwick Water and the Crawfurdland Water flow, merging to become the Kilmarnock Water.

Kilmarnock grew from the weaving industry; the first factory was built by a group of local merchants in 1746. Later, during the nineteenth century, the woollen industry flourished with the development of machines used to manufacture shawls and bonnets – the famous 'Kilmarnock Bunnets'. The whisky-blending industry had its early beginnings in Kilmarnock by Johnnie Walker, 'born in 1820 and still growing strong'.

The town has had a long association with Robert Burns, since the first edition of his poems – 'the Kilmarnock Edition' – was published there. A monument to him was erected in 1879 in Kay Park and the Burns Federation was formed in 1885, with 49 affiliated clubs being set up all over the country.

Whilst in Kilmarnock it is worth going to see the Dick Institute in Bank Avenue, close to the academy. This neo-classical building was presented to the town by James Dick who made a fortune out of the commercial use of gutta-percha, a substance resembling rubber. The institute houses the town's main library and a museum and art gallery.

Kilmarnock today still has a thriving industrial base and is the only place left in Scotland which still manufactures locomotives. Johnnie Walker also built a new blending and bottling plant there in the 1950s.

The centre of the town is now mostly pedestrianised, so getting about has become much easier. The disused railway starts again two miles or so to the east of Kilmarnock. If you leave the town by Bonnington Road and then turn left on to the B751 in the direction of Kilmaurs, the dismantled railway starts again to the north of Knockentibber and continues to Irvine. This line would make an ideal cycleway, joining the Clyde Cycleway (after its completion) with Irvine, and when the link to Stranraer is built, that will form a route all the way to Ireland.